D090350

D... D...
the deserted stage

24515

Oakton Community College
Morton Grove, Illinois

THE DESERTED STAGE

THE
DESERTED STAGE

The Search for Dramatic Form
in Nineteenth-Century
England

By Terry Otten

Ohio University Press/Athens

TO ROMA A. KING, JR.

CONTENTS

Introduction   3

CHAPTER 1. Shelley's *The Cenci*   13

CHAPTER 2. Byron's *Cain* and *Werner*   41

CHAPTER 3. Tennyson's *Maud* and *Becket*   76

CHAPTER 4. Browning's *A Blot in the 'Scutcheon* and
            Pippa Passes   108

CHAPTER 5. End and Beginning   143

Notes   150

Bibliography   160

Index   173

ACKNOWLEDGMENTS

I am first and foremost indebted to my good wife Jane.

I thank the Board of College Education of the Lutheran Church in America for a generous stipend which freed me from teaching responsibilities in order to complete the manuscript.

I am grateful to Atheneum Publishers for permission to quote from Loren Eiseley's *The Firmament of Time* (Copyright 1960 by Loren Eiseley and The Trustees of the University of Pennsylvania) and to the editors of *Research Studies* and *The Bucknell Review* for permissions to use certain portions of my essays published in their journals in 1968 and 1969.

I especially thank my very generous readers and critics: Hill Shine, Professor Emeritus of the University of Kentucky; James N. Thompson and Frank B. Fieler of Ohio University; Allen J. Koppenhaver and John W. Ostrom of Wittenberg University.

To Roma A. King, Jr., I owe a debt not easily repaid. I gladly dedicate this book to him.

THE DESERTED STAGE

The great stage . . . the world stage where
the Elizabethans saw us strutting and
mouthing our parts, has the skeletons of
dead actors under the floor boards, and the
dusty scenery of forgotten dramas lies
abandoned in the wings. The idea necessarily comes home to us then with a sudden
chill: What if we are not playing on the
center stage? What if the Great Spectacle
has no terminus and no meaning? What if
there is no audience beyond the footlights,
and the play, in spite of bold villains and
posturing heroes, is a shabby repeat per-
formance in an echoing vacuity?

LOREN EISELEY *The Firmament of Time*

INTRODUCTION

Content presents the task; form, the solution.
                              Frederich Hebbel, *Journals*

Defending the relevance of nineteenth-century English drama seems as hopeless as defending Benedict Arnold before the Daughters of the American Revolution. Never have so many major authors contributed so little to the history of English drama. Despite the fact that every major nineteenth-century poet wrote dramas and almost all of them condemned the current stage, not one could rescue the theater from senile plots, pseudo-Elizabethan techniques, melodramatic claptrap, stock characterizations, and bombastic language. Moreover, these literary giants contributed to rather than arrested the decline and committed the further offense of forever sentencing unsuspecting graduate students and literary coroners to the odious chore of exhuming the corpse. How it was possible for such poets to produce a body of dramas so bad has baffled more than one critic.

I am concerned here both with explaining the cause of their failure and, more importantly, with defining the limits of their success—for in point of fact significant plays were written during the nineteenth century. These works pointed drama in a new direction, even though none of them was produced on the contemporary stage or directly influenced the development of drama in that century. In retrospect, we may speak of two kinds of nineteenth-century drama: conventional popular plays performed in the theaters and experimental dramas composed by major poets. The first requires no explanation and merits no defense; the second warrants both.

Most critics theorize that the depraved condition of the theater itself was largely responsible for the failure of established poets to write acceptable plays. Political circumstances and censorship, theater architecture, audience behavior, theatrical managers, middle-class taste, the star system, staging practices, and the absence of constructive criticism have all been blamed for the decay of English drama. Some historians accuse the poets of refusing to acknowledge stage restrictions; others suggest that neither the writers nor the age was suited to drama.[1] Although something of truth may exist in all these explanations, the underlying crucial cause was something else: a new concept of reality created a serious structural impasse.

A distrust of *a priori* principles as the basis of truth led to "the awakening of the modern spirit" at the dawning of the nineteenth century. The eighteenth-century rationalist had found God through reason; the romantic found him by developing his own self-awareness. Coleridge wrote in the *Biographia Literaria*, "The act of self-consciousness is for us the source and principle of all our knowledge." At midcentury Matthew Arnold could say with painful certainty, "the calm, the cheerfulness, the disinterested objectivity have disappeared: the dialogue of the mind with itself has commenced; modern problems have presented themselves; we hear already the doubts; we witness the discouragements, of Hamlet and of Faust" (Preface to *Poems*, 1853). In rejecting eighteenth-century empiricism and positing the self as the center of reality, nineteenth-century writers necessarily discarded conventional artistic forms. Traditional modes of understanding were no longer functional in light of the intellectual and cultural revolution taking place.[2] The romantic poets transformed lyric poetry, the ode, the sonnet, the romance tale, the elegy, the epic, into subjective visions of reality. The novel rapidly rose to prominence as a medium capable of depicting the "inwardness" of characters. What of drama?

Traditional drama, like the epic, embodies communal values and beliefs. It assumes an order beyond characters, following a transcendent pattern of ritual, whether based on religious belief like Greek or Elizabethan drama or on "the order of things" like the syllogistic structures of Racine and Corneille. On the contrary, romantic literature, August Wilhelm Schlegel was to say, "is the expression of the secret attraction to a chaos which is concealed beneath the regulated creation even in its very bosom, and . . . is perpetually striving after new and wonderful births."[3] Bringing such a literature to life on the stage proved exceedingly difficult. The experimental dramas I shall treat in this study show that the dramatists in question consciously or unconsciously redefined action in drama, seeing it, as Schlegel said, as "an activity dependent upon the will of man, . . . a new definition in the conception of action, namely, the reference to the idea of moral liberty, by which alone man is considered as the first author of his determination."[4] Reversing, thereby, the long-accepted Aristotelian priorities, nineteenth-century writers made character rather than plot the soul of action. In the concluding chapter of his important book *The Poetry of Experience: The Dramatic Monologue in Modern Literary Tradition*, Robert Langbaum describes the result of that reversal in poetry:

> The poetry of experience breaks through the Aristotelian succession of events to achieve the condition of the lyric. And it is by violating the Aristotelian rules for achieving logical completeness or limited meaning that it breaks through. Yet the poem remains both dramatic and lyrical because it must be dramatic in order to be lyrical—because it uses limited meaning, if not to resolve the poem, then at least as an event in the poem, an event to be dissolved in the tide of unlimited meaning.[5]

In drama as well, the ascendancy of character, with an accompanying sense of incompleteness and relativity, generated the need for new or revised forms; but recognized dramatic structure proved less pliable than conventional poetic modes.

Where was a suitable structural model in drama to be found?

Many romantic idolaters of Shakespeare thought that he might serve—but only because they reinterpreted him in their own terms. Beginning as early as Maurice Morgann's famous *Essay on the Dramatic Character of John Falstaff* (1777), critics admired Shakespeare primarily for his ability to create character. In his attempt to study the *"whole* character of Falstaff," Morgann virtually ignored plot for the sake of character. Charles Lamb conceived of Shakespeare's heroes as enormously complex character studies almost independent of the stage. The mind of King Lear is "laid bare" with such devastating power, he wrote, that the play is unactable (*On the Tragedies of Shakespeare, Considered with Reference to Their Fitness for Stage Presentation*, 1811). Coleridge's famous theory of Hamlet's "overbalance of imaginative power" (*Lectures of 1818*) is less a comment on the play than a psychological reading of the character's modernity. Hazlitt, too, spotlighted character at the expense of plot in *Characters of Shakespeare's Plays* (1817). A. C. Bradley, epitomizing the nineteenth-century interpretation of Shakespearean drama in his influential *Shakespearian Tragedy* (1904), recorded his impressions of the tragedies "as records of what passed in the minds of Shakespeare and of the characters."[6]

When nineteenth-century writers projected their romantic sensibility into Shakespearean dramas, they saw the realistic portrayal of subjective reality as the *force majeure* of the action. They misread Shakespeare because they tended to forgo plot for character, whereas Shakespeare was always ultimately concerned with the working out of plot, in spite of his attempts to link character to action. Shakespeare's characters never quite attain separate identities outside the requirements of plot; they exist in a world dominated by superhuman forces. Shakespeare "embraces reality but he transcends it," Erich Auerbach has shown:

> This is already apparent in the presence of ghosts and witches in his plays, and in the often unrealistic style. . . .
> It is still more significantly revealed in the inner structure of the action which is often . . . only erratically and sporadically realistic and often shows a tendency to break through into

the realm of the fairy tale, of playful fancy, or of the supernatural and demonic. . . . He does not take ordinary everyday reality seriously or tragically. He treats only noblemen,
princes, and kings, statesmen, commanders, and antique
heroes tragically.[7]

Influenced by earlier German thought, Coleridge developed a
theory of organic structure which reversed the Aristotelian priorities. This theory of dramatic action invalidates the view that
character is subordinate to plot. Rather than being the agent of
the action, character constitutes the action. Consequently, Coleridge could say of classical literature, "The Greeks changed the
ideas into infinities, and these finites into *anthropomorphi*, or
forms of men. . . . With them form was the end." In contrast,
modern literature achieves an opposite effect "by turning the
mind inward on its essence instead of letting it act only on its
outward circumstances and communities. . . . And it is this sub-
jectivity which principally and most fundamentally distinguishes
all classic from all the modern poetry" (*Lectures of 1818*). Viewing Shakespeare as a modern playwright, he contended, "His
characters are never introduced for the sake of his plot, but his
plot arises out of his characters."[8] The order of his dramas
"grows and evolves itself from within," he reasoned in the closing lecture of his 1818 series; and he praised Shakespeare for
"Independence of the interest on the story as the groundwork
of plot." Coleridge differentiated between action and story, noting that what happens externally in a play is not as important as
what happens internally: Shakespeare's drama "shapes, as it develops, itself from within. . . ." For Coleridge, as for the other
romantic critics of Shakespeare, plot was the adjunct of character
rather than its determinant. The dynamic organizing principle of
drama became "Action in Character, rather than Character in
Action," as Browning was to put it in the 1837 preface to *Strafford.*
Adopting Elizabethan dramaturgy to express modern subjective matter was too much like grafting an alien myth onto a new
vision. The modern concern with the individual and the internal

"dialogue of the mind with itself" worked at odds with a communal drama directed to a homogeneous body of believers. Even though there is much more emphasis on characters as individuals in Shakespearean drama than in Greek drama, ritual is always apparent and plot ultimately dominates character. In both classical and Elizabethan drama, "the very nature of unity or order presupposes for its delineation an ordered approach, an approach, in fact, which necessitates rules."[9] With the new emphasis on character, on multiple aspects of one's experience, drama was no longer solely addressed to an audience attuned to the mythic implications of plot or common moral and ethical themes. Rather than affirming social and moral law, the character was now often engaged in a struggle to erect a morality within himself to counter the metaphysical dissolution he witnessed everywhere around him. Existence lacked solidarity, and action in drama ceased to move directly to an "appointed end." Instead of being an arrangement of incidents toward a given end, action acquired a new dimension: character often denied the resolution of external conflicts. Flaubert could speak of an "art without conclusions." Continuous narrative plot structured on a causal pattern was no longer possible or relevant.

For an older Matthew Arnold grown weary of the "multitudinousness" of his age, social and moral decay meant the demise of drama. "In England we have no drama at all," he announced in 1879. "Our vast society is not homogeneous enough, not sufficiently united, even any large portion of it, in a common view of life, a common ideal capable of serving as basis for a modern English drama" ("French Play in London"). In our own century Irving Babbitt has judged the substance of romantic literature ephemeral in that the romantic's imagination "is not drawn back to any ethical centre, and so is free to wander wild in its own empire of chimeras."[10] He is describing in fact not what the romantics chose to do with the imagination but what they had to do. He misses the important point that the wandering itself is a search for form, an appendage of the *Weltanschauung*. Far from permitting the free reign of the imagination, the romantics employed it in the search for some "ethical centre." They knew only too well that they lacked a "centre," and they conceived of action in drama not so much as the individual's retreat from fixed moral and ethical values as his continuous search for a metaphysical resolve which was neither definable nor certain. In this respect romantic literature is nearly always dramatic because it is both dialectical and dynamic. Its very essence is subjective conflict and action. Its aim is structure. Friedrich Schlegel identified an ensuing tension between matter and form implicit in modern literature in his youthful essay on Greek poetry written in 1795-1796:

> Die Bildungsgeschichte der modernen Poesie stellt nichts andres dar, als den staten Streit der subjektiven Anlage, und der objektiven Tendenz des ästhetischen Vermögens und das allmählige Uebergewicht des letztern.[11]

And yet if the new literature aims at structure, it paradoxically defies completion or permanence of form—"The formulation is that the formulation itself must never be allowed to settle into dogma."[12]

The problem then is structure—the conflict between subjective matter and objective form. For all its protestations of independence, nineteenth-century English drama was founded on structural formulas. Popular stage melodrama, brought into England via the German playwright Kotzebue (1761-1819), depended on stock ingredients: a heavy Gothic setting, an improbable plot pitting a perfect hero against a despicable villain, an orphaned heroine (usually reunited with her father), and a moral resolution with the proper dispensation of reward and punishment. Verse drama wedded Shakespearean poetry to the Gothic pattern: characters were all but obscured by setting, or they were reduced to passions so extreme and to remorse so agonizing that their pitiable states affected "a true Aristotelian catharsis, enabling the spectator to save himself from destruction" by holding his emotions in check.[13] The introduction of the French well-made play led to a structure even more rigidly defined. A host of historical and domestic plays followed the meticulously prescribed formula of the *pièce bien faite*. The nineteenth-century English theater was a buyer's market, and the commodity in demand was a drama traditional enough or superficial enough to be within the grasp of its clientele.

Any poet who would translate his modern poetic vision into drama had to seek unity in something other than Aristotelian plot structure. He had to discover a new expressive form capable of reflecting his interest in subjective reality. Facing a theater which afforded no opportunity for experimentation and an audience not interested in serious drama, he could reject the actual stage and compose a closet drama or adjust his play to the demands of the current theater. Either way he was almost certain to fail, in the first case because he was groping toward an unrealized and untestable stage form, and in the second case because accepted stage practices worked against the new drama of character. Nonetheless, major poets did grapple with the problem of form, as experimental dramas written in the century demonstrate.

In order to describe the new subjectivism in drama and to explain the playwright's difficulty with form, I have examined representative plays by four distinguished poets: Shelley, Byron, Tennyson, and Browning. I have chosen these writers because all of them not only succeeded in innovating structural patterns in poetry but also tried, by different means, to write viable drama. With the exception of the chapter on Shelley, I examine two plays by each author, one demonstrating his use of traditional form, the other his attempt to evolve a new kind of structure, to show that the degree of success or failure of each play may be measured by the writer's ability to embody subjective action in dramatic form.

Shelley's only stage play, *The Cenci*, demonstrates in one play the contrasting poles of the new and the old drama. Externally, *The Cenci* typifies the pseudo-Elizabethan dramas of the romantic age; internally, it is a modern study of action in character. In choosing to model his play after his conception of Shakespearean drama, Shelley was following a stage convention he assumed appropriate to his purpose. But an implicit conflict between the plot and the emerging subjective action in character almost fractures the play. Attempting to "make apparent some of the most dark and secret caverns of the human heart," Shelley unconsciously exceeded the restrictions of the structural model he followed.

Byron wore more than one dramatic mask. Save for *Werner*, which imitates the pyrotechnics of contemporary melodramas, Byron vacillated between neoclassicism and romanticism in writing his plays, arguing for the unities in "regular" plays on the one hand and abandoning almost all stage conventions in his "metaphysical" plays on the other. *Cain* is the most modern of his plays both in its iconoclastic view of Cain as a revolutionary hero and in the subjective nature of the action. Using as a structural base the inversion of Christian myth, Byron sought to portray a new concept of morality centered in character, a "mental theatre." Seeing it in juxtaposition with *Werner* illustrates the wide dissimilarity between a popular drama in decay and a modern drama being born.

To Tennyson the difference between subjective matter and objective dramatic form was so great that he never considered synthesis possible. When he finally wrote for the stage near the end of his career, he followed the leadership of Henry Irving, the great Shakespeare worshiper, and imitated Elizabethan models. And yet Tennyson's best poetry contains subjective dramatic movement characteristic of the emerging modern drama. The best example of his ability to depict such action is *Maud*, a monodrama which Tennyson thought "slightly akin to 'Hamlet' . . . where successive phases of passion *in one person* take the place of successive persons." In discussing the concept of action in *Maud* and the action and form of *Becket*, a late play in ancient dress, I hope to differentiate between traditional and modern dramatic action and to demonstrate Tennyson's structural difficulty in projecting his modern view of character on a stage.

More than any of the other poets, Robert Browning was consciously aware of the problem of dramatic form. Unlike Tennyson, he thought drama a proper vehicle for describing internal action in character, at least until his experiences alienated him

11

from the stage. He probably knew the theater more intimately than the other three poets mentioned and for a longer time devoted his energies to writing for the stage. In composing *A Blot in the 'Scutcheon* Browning integrated Elizabethan plot structure and the devices of the "well-made" play. As a result an elaborate exterior form obscures the underlying dramatic conflict in character. In *Pippa Passes*, however, he consciously tried to erect a form suited to his modern concept of action and character. The play is a daring experimental drama in its form and matter—and very nearly a successful stage piece.

Briefly stated, the thesis of this book is this: the primarily subjective or internal action in each play forced its poet to experiment with new structural forms or drastically to modify orthodox dramatic form. My purpose is to explain each poet's achievement or lack of it in terms of structure. My approach will be to differentiate between the external plot and the internal movement—that is, the "Action in Character," the emotional and intellectual emergence of character—and to suggest the main outlines of a new dramatic form toward which the plays move.

I need to define briefly what I mean by certain critical terms. I use the word *action* to identify the central dramatic movement of the play. There are two levels of movement in the dramas: an external development, or *plot*, by which I mean the chronological arrangement of incidents; and an internal development, by which I mean the essential *action in character*. Similarly, there are two kinds of conflict, one lying outside of character and one residing within character. In the experimental dramas the *outer* or *external conflict* (Beatrice Cenci versus her father, Cain versus his family and the tyrant God, Maud's lover versus her brother) is superseded by *inner* or *internal conflict* within character. In each of these plays a dialectical as opposed to chronological pattern evolves which both determines and unifies the dramatic movement.

1

SHELLEY'S *THE CENCI*

La nature de l'amour-propre et de ce *moi* humain est de n'aimer
que soi et de ne considérer que soi. Mais que fera-t-il? Il ne
saurait empêcher que cet objet qu'il aime ne soit plein de
défauts et de misères: il veut être grand, et il se voit petit;
il veut être heureux, et il se voit misérable; il veut être parfait,
et il se voit plein d'imperfections; il veut être l'objet de l'amour
et de l'estime des hommes, et il voit que ses défauts ne méritent
que leur aversion et leur mépris. Cet embarras où il se trouve
produit en lui la plus injuste et la plus criminelle passion
qu'il soit possible de s'imaginer; car il conçoit une haine
mortelle contre cette vérité que le reprend, et qui le convainc
de ses défauts.

PASCAL *Pensées*

The Cenci has appealed to many critics and convinced almost
none. Though brilliant in its poetic effects, the critics say, it is deficient as drama. Fit less for the stage than the study, *The Cenci*
is an attractive bastard. Moody Prior identifies its illegitimacy in
The Language of Tragedy: "*The Cenci* is an impressive work, but
it is not great drama, not merely because Shelley lacked the requi-
site training in the mechanics of the form, but because he wrote
primarily as a lyric poet."[1] The ground of Prior's assumption will
not allow him to give Shelley his due as dramatist, for he applies
an essentially Aristotelian concept of tragedy to Shelley's play.

Granting his implicit theory that lyric drama cannot be staged, he can only find Shelley wanting as a dramatist, however regretfully he may pass judgment.

But is it possible that Shelley, perhaps unconsciously, was moving toward a new kind of drama, a drama which by the end of the century was to find full expression in Ibsen's late symbolic dramas and Strindberg's expressionistic dream plays? If Shelley failed, he did so not because his vision was somehow undramatic but because he sensed intuitively that the dramatic center should lie elsewhere than in narrative or plot, that is, "the soul of the action" in Aristotelian form. As a result, he came very close to creating a successful drama of character, primarily subjective in nature, while, at the same time, he imitated drama of plot, the sole structural model inherited from the tradition of English drama. In attempting to construct his play within the confines of a traditional structure, Shelley created a modern drama in ancient dress.

Not that he was necessarily aware of the iconoclastic nature of the play or of its inappropriateness to the nineteenth-century English stage. He wrote to Thomas Love Peacock that *The Cenci* was "done in two months, was a fine antidote to nervous medicines and kept up, I think, the pain in my side, as sticks do a fire."[2] And although he thought the play "singularly fitted for the stage," he had made no real effort to learn staging practices before he wrote it. The prejudice he held against the popular stage, which Peacock speaks about in his *Memoirs of Percy Bysshe Shelley*, kept him from the theater throughout his life. In her journal Mary Shelley frequently refers to attending operas and plays, but she almost never mentions Shelley in connection with the stage. Even in her note to *The Cenci* she admits that although Shelley "wished *The Cenci* to be acted," he himself "was not a playgoer, being of such fastidious taste that he was easily disgusted by the bad filling up of inferior parts."[3] Despite his disdain of the contemporary stage, however, Shelley said *The Cenci* was "expressly written for theatrical exhibition," and he stated explicitly in his letter of instruction to Peacock that the play was to be presented at Covent Garden with Eliza O'Neill cast in the role of Beatrice—"it might even seem to have been written for her" (*Works* 10:62). Ignorant though he was about the stage, he really believed the play suited for the "popular" taste. He confessed to its conventionality and considered it uncharacteristic of his own style, a play "totally in a different style from anything I have yet composed" (*Works* 10:79).

But even if Shelley naively sought to accommodate himself to the demands of the current theater, he took up writing about Beatrice Cenci in earnest. He was fascinated by her strange story and by Guido's supposed portrait of her. And, although he sometimes spoke derisively of *The Cenci* when he measured it against his higher mission as artist, he defended it against his critics as a "work of art" and unashamedly aligned himself with "Sophocles, Massinger, Voltaire and Alfieri . . . Good Heavens, what would they have tragedy!" (*Works* 10:171). Furthermore, Shelley was too devoted to his art, too committed to his task as "unacknowledged legislator" not to have taken the substance of the story seriously. The "sad reality" which he found in Beatrice engaged his sympathy—"the image of Beatrice haunted me after seeing her portrait."[4] Shelley was not prostituting his art in writing the play, it seems, but exploring a new medium with much self-consciousness and uncertainty. Knowing that the play represented a departure from his usual writing, "a work of art . . . not coloured by my feelings, nor obscured by my metaphysics,"[5] he was reluctant to make any high claims for it. And yet he thought enough of it to define its intent in a carefully worded preface and to respond to critical attacks.

What is so revolutionary about the play? If it is different from Shelley's more "visionary" poetry, it appears to be traditional enough as drama. His contemporaries saw nothing new about it, even if they recognized its achievement. Peacock, for example, thought it would have been "a great work in the days of Massinger," but he judged it deficient for "the modern English stage. . . . [Shelley] could not clip his wings to the littleness of the acting drama."[6] Such judgment is still being passed. A. M. D. Hughes pays it the almost backhanded compliment of calling it "the finest example of the tragedy of criminal passion in the tall Elizabethan manner since Ford relinquished it."[7] And Edmund Blunden has theorized that if Shelley had only decided "not to wear the dowdy costume" of Elizabethan drama and had found "a fresh style and attire for his play of Beatrice . . . what a rejection he could have ensured for it at the great theatres, and what a play posterity would possess!"[8] But as Seymour Reiter points out in *A Study of Shelley's Poetry*, it is totally unfair to "accuse Shelley of imitativeness in an age when formal originality would have made production a vain hope."[9] Perhaps more important, we must ask what dramatic models Shelley might have used even if he had realized that he could not have the play staged. His dilemma was not that the contemporary stage accepted only the pattern of pseudo-Elizabethan drama but that he had no other structural types to imitate and no means of experimenting with dramatic form on a stage. Furthermore, Shelley's own close reading of Sophocles, Shakespeare, and Calderón inhibited his vision. We sometimes forget that a modern dramatist writes with over a hundred-and-fifty years of experimental drama behind him, whereas the romantic poets were caught between a moribund dramatic tradition and the development of new dramatic forms not yet conceivable on the English stage. Shelley used Elizabethan dramaturgy not because he hoped to make the play acceptable to the current stage but because he could see no alternative.

Unfortunately, critics have largely ignored Shelley's perceptive comments on the nature of dramatic form; but his criticism comes very close to describing the artistic impasse he faced when he turned to the stage. In the first place, Shelley anticipated that critics would object to his lyricism in drama. He believed *The Cenci* fit for the stage in part because it described "passions I have never felt" and told "the most dreadful story in pure and refined language."[10] In contrast, he admitted that a work like *Hellas* could not be staged. Yet he still employed dramatic form even when acknowledging in the preface that "The subject in its present state is unsusceptible of being treated otherwise than lyrically. . . ." He was unable to label *Hellas* a true drama, but he felt somehow that it should be. He seemed to be groping toward some reconciliation between lyric poetry, which he recognized as subjective, and dramatic form, which he recognized as objective. It is not without significance that when Browning in his *Essay on Shelley* tried to envision a new drama, he imagined an artist who could combine the art of Shakespeare and Shelley.

Furthermore, Shelley was remarkably incisive in discussing the particular problem confronting a poet who would copy traditional drama. The "form" of drama can be imitated, he suggested in the preface to *Prometheus Unbound*, but the "spirit" cannot. He firmly believed that traditional drama was the manifestation of the social entity, a communal art in the fullest sense. Greek drama, he noted in the *Defence of Poetry*, produced a "common effect" of "language, action, music, painting, the dance, and religious institutions." But the modern age is fragmented. The modern actor cannot even wear a "mask" because our system of acting "is favourable only to a partial and inharmonious effect; it is fit for nothing but a monologue. . . ." Shelley is suggesting something more than that the "system" of acting is faulty. He implies, regretfully to be sure, that the loss of the mask symbolizes the loss of communal values. By contrast, the monologue implies that value resides less in what the actor represents in his ritualistic role than what he himself conveys as truth on the stage. Character, in other words, becomes increasingly autonomous. Significantly, Shelley did not argue that modern dramatists should write as the ancients. He condemned Calderón, whom he admired, precisely because Calderón tried to connect drama and religion, music and dance. Such an attempt is doomed to failure, he concluded, "by a substitution of rigidly-defined and ever-repeated idealisms of a distorted superstition for the living impersonation of the truth of human passions."

For Greek and Elizabethan audiences holding to a common body of beliefs, a drama of ritual was both justified and appropriate. Tragedy embodied communal values in the form of visualized myths. One reason why Shelley and the other romantics turned back to Shakespeare was no doubt the belief that tragic drama could be restored only on the grounds of a universality they found lacking in their own age. Their interest in Shakespeare, like the broad interest in resurrecting old myths in the modern period generally, was partly motivated by an intense desire to recover a lost order. Shelley knew, however, that drama could never again be the same as it was to the Greeks and Elizabethans: "But in periods of the decay of social life, the drama sympathizes with that decay. Tragedy becomes a cold imitation of the form of the great masterpieces of antiquity, divested of all harmonious accompaniment of the kindred arts and often the very form misunderstood . . ." (*The Defence of Poetry*).

In effect, to imitate the form of traditional tragedy when the system of values implied by the form is dissolved can lead only to a kind of spurious Apollonian art. For Shelley the early nineteenth century, bereft of a clearly defined morality and hidebound to a decadent and dying religious institution, seemed particularly unfit for classical tragedy. Nonetheless, he sensed, if he did not completely understand why, that drama was possible. He looked to Byron to substitute "something worthy of the English stage, for the miserable trash which, from Milman to Barry Cornwall, has been intruded on it since the demand for tragical representation" (*Works* 10:265). Moreover, he did not hesitate to defend his own stage play. His detestation of the current theater and more essentially his theory that tragedy was not possible in an age of "social decay" seem contradictory to his desire to write a "tragedy" about Beatrice Cenci; but Shelley adjusted the structural demands of a traditional tragedy to a modern view of character and so unwittingly reinterpreted the meaning of tragedy itself.

The preface to *The Cenci* implies a primary shift in focus from Elizabethan-Aristotelian drama, for Shelley emphasizes character as the primary interest of the play. He informs the reader that the tragedy had "already received . . . approbation and success. Nothing remained . . . but to clothe it to the apprehension of my countrymen in such language and action as would bring it home to their hearts." According to Mary Shelley's note, Shelley had little interest in the construction of plot and felt himself deficient in "forming and following up a story," but the record of Count Cenci's murder was already predetermined by the historical documents Shelley received. Consequently, the fertile ground for Shelley's imagination lay primarily in character. He was free to explore character without being distracted by the need to invent the narrative line of the play. In effect Shelley attempted to draw out of the surface action of the historical plot the significance of the characters who shaped the events. Action in character could therefore coexist with character in action, and Shelley was not hindered from impersonating "my own apprehension of the beautiful and the just" or probing the dark unknown in character. In consequence, the characters in the drama overshadowed the historical events. Beatrice is distinctly different from the typical Aristotelian protagonist. Not an agent of plot or a ritualistic scapegoat doomed to self-sacrifice for the redemption of society, she attains a measure of autonomy beyond the traditional tragic hero. Standing outside rather than within the framework of a communal moral code, she is a modern heroine as much akin to Ibsen's protagonists as to Shakespeare's. In discussing the theological revolution taking place in the romantic period, Northrup Frye, in *A Study of Romanticism*, accounts for the new definition of character and action in drama:

> In pre-Romantic imagery the world of social and civilized life, however evil and corrupt, and however thoroughly denounced, was still the gateway to identity: man for pre-Romantic poets was still primarily a social and civilized being and could not progress except through his social heritage. In a great deal of Romantic imagery human society is thought of as leading to alienation rather than identity, and this sense increases steadily throughout the nineteenth century as literature becomes more ironic in both tone and structure.[11]

Elizabethan in its dress but modern in its matter, *The Cenci* delineates the unrelenting struggle of Beatrice Cenci to place herself within a social and moral context no longer valid.

In a way the preface divides the interest between what lies within and without character. On one hand, Shelley highlights the tyranny of Count Cenci, the immorality of the church, and the impotence of the social community, all of which lead Beatrice to murder her father "by the necessity of circumstances and opinions." On the other hand, he speaks of another concern when he argues that the play "would be as a light to make apparent some of the most dark and secret caverns of the human heart." The tyranny outside the self is juxtaposed with a more devastating tyranny within it. The play itself projects this dualism. As a consequence critics have tended either to reduce *The Cenci* to a simplistic Elizabethan-Gothic horror story or, considering the radical reversal in Beatrice's character soon after she is raped, to condemn it as a hopelessly divided play.[12] The apparent structural difficulties, however, stem from Shelley's attempt to expose Beatrice's character as she moves in an almost Blakean sense from innocence to experience. At times the sensational Elizabethan plot, with its Gothic morbidity and darkness, simultaneously obscures the drama within character, and provides a concatenation of events, a caricature of "evil," and a pervasive gloom that consistently project and define a drama of self.

Seymour Reiter has offered the best analysis of the structure of the play in *A Study of Shelley's Poetry*.[13] He contends convincingly that the play contains a beginning, middle, and end designating the major changes in Beatrice's "condition." Whereas I believe he is completely accurate in seeing Beatrice as the structural center of the action, I feel he places undue emphasis on Beatrice's deteriorating situation. The disintegration of Beatrice's world, which composes the *plot* of the play, is more the catalyst than the end of the *action*. The structure stems from the character, not the plot. To account for the structural pattern in the play, we must probe Beatrice's subconscious motivations as well as describe the changing "conditions" in which she finds herself.

The action may be summarized briefly as follows. In the first two acts the movement is essentially external—Cenci initiates his attack on Beatrice with veiled references to the impending incest. He is the aggressor, Beatrice the passive recipient. At this point the play seems a stock Gothic horror tale; but as Shelley depicts Beatrice's increasing isolation, he establishes the grounds for the internal action which is to follow. We sense that Beatrice's goodness impinges primarily on her allegiance to an externally applied morality, that her strength and justification come from something outside herself. The rape precipitates a dramatic shift in her behavior, not because of the physical fact of rape but because of Beatrice's mistaken assumption that her innocence has been violated. Believing that her innocence, the last and strongest line in her defense against her father's evil, has been endangered by the incest, she fights back to preserve her purity. She begins to play her father's role: symbolically, she becomes her "father's child." Now the aggressor rather than the helpless victim, Beatrice battles to maintain her innocence—only to reenact her father's guilt. Having conceived a moral hatred against the "truth" which condemns her of her fault, to apply Pascal, she commits the "pernicious mistake" of cold-blooded murder. The last act then begins with her spurious, but not inappropriate, defense of herself in court and ends with self-recognition, however limited. In her confrontation with reality, Beatrice discovers a new source of strength within herself. Each of these developments needs to be described in detail.

On the surface, the first two acts consist of flat characterization and improbable incidents. Cenci's sadistic nature is caricatured, and the plot increases in intensity as it moves steadily toward the rape at the beginning of Act 3. Cenci's hints at incest in Act 1 (i.140-41; iii.169-72) become overt threats in Act 2 when Beatrice frantically tells her stepmother Lucretia that Cenci spoke only "one word, Mother, one little word; / One look; one smile." As scene two ends, Cenci finally determines to "walk secure and unbeheld / Toward my purpose!" Everything points to the "rape of innocence." In fact, the plot seems too contrived, the characters too melodramatic, the conflict too simplistic. Viewed as a conventional Gothic thriller, such as those popular just prior to

Shelley's writing the play, *The Cenci* holds no particular attraction, except that the poetry, as Moody Prior has observed, is distinguished by its "high degree of intensity and feeling." But even in the conventional Gothic plot, Shelley initiates subtle structural patterns in the first two acts which make the play something more than what it seems.

The basic conflict, for example, is superficially the life-and-death struggle between Cenci and Beatrice. But Shelley stresses the ambiguous nature of the combatants. Count Cenci is so excessive a caricature, so totally unrealistic that Shelley must have conceived of him as less a character than a monomaniacal fiend set loose upon the world. And yet precisely because he is more a force than a character, Count Cenci renders judgment impossible and meaningless. Like a grotesque figure out of the Theater of Cruelty, this "dark spirit" knows neither bounds nor pretense. Consequently, in the first scene when Cenci discusses with Camillo his successful attempt to buy the pope's favor, he illuminates the church's guilt rather than his own. Measured against the calculating avarice of the church, Cenci's evil is almost excusable. He has no alternative; he is an "abandoned fiend" compelled by some force he can neither identify nor control. It is not enough to call him a typical "Shelleyan villain." The composite guilt of the cowardly social community, the opportunistic Orsino, the pope, and the church in general is far less pardonable.

Cenci is a simplistic or whole character but nonetheless an ambivalent figure with something of the duplicity characteristic of the Gothic villain. Delighting in the exquisite "luxury" of torture, he tells Camillo that he pursues the soul: "I rarely kill the body, which preserves, / Like a strong prison, the soul within my power. . . ." Attracted by "a deed . . . / Whose horror might make sharp an appetite / Duller than mine," he warns Beatrice of "a charm [that] shall make thee meek and tame." Unmistakably, he is incited by a compulsion to shatter Beatrice's will, to destroy her very being:

> Come darkness! Yet, what is the day to me?
> And wherefore should I wish for night, who does

> A deed which shall confound both night and day?
> 'Tis she shall grope through a bewildering mist
> Of horror: if there be a sun in heaven
> She shall not dare to look upon its beams;
> Nor feel its warmth. Let her then wish for night.
> (II.i.181-87)

He rejects physical violence as an end and employs it as a means. The value of incest is that it jeopardizes the purity which gives Beatrice temporary superiority of will. The question is not whether Cenci can subjugate Beatrice's body but whether he can invade the fortress of her supposed innocence.

By utilizing another of the conventional qualities of the Gothic villain, Shelley again hints at Cenci's ambiguity. In the banquet scene in which he gleefully announces the deaths of his sons Christafano and Rocco, Cenci concludes that "Heaven has special care of me." In melodramatically allowing "most favouring Providence" to bring about the deaths, Shelley seems bent on establishing the ambiguity of divine power itself. He juxtaposes Cenci's God with Beatrice's. Beatrice later exonerates her act of murder on the grounds of carrying out God's will, just as Cenci lays claim to Heaven's favor in the improbable deaths of his sons. He pledges himself to dark powers:

> Oh, thou bright wine whose purple splendour leaps
> And bubbles gaily in this golden bowl
> Under the lamplight, as my spirits do,
> To hear the death of my accursed sons!
> Could I believe thou wert their mingled blood,
> Then would I taste thee like a sacrament,
> And pledge with thee the mighty Devil in Hell,
> Who, if a father's curses, as men say,
> Climb with swift wings after their children's souls,
> And drag them from the very throne of Heaven,
> Now triumphs in my triumph!   (I.iii.76-86)

But if his vow to Satanic forces leads to revenge, so does Beatrice's devotion to the God of justice. Cenci's demonic worship of God and Beatrice's orthodox absolutism are ironically parallel, and Shelley fully exploits the similarities later in the play.

Beatrice's character is far more complex than Cenci's and far less exposed in the first two acts. Cenci tells his purpose at the beginning of the play and does not deviate from it. In denying the development of Cenci as a character, Shelley places emphasis on the evolution of his heroine. In order to catch the important aspects of her nature as Shelley reveals them gradually in the first two acts, we must follow her through each of the scenes. She is first mentioned in scene one, when Camillo makes the totally ironic comment to Cenci, "Methinks her sweet looks, which make all things else / Beauteous and glad, might kill the fiend within you." In point of fact, Cenci "kills" the innocence of Beatrice; but until Beatrice engineers the murder, she appears the epitome of virtue.

Shelley uses the sinister Orsino to characterize Beatrice much as he employs Camillo to reveal Cenci. Just as Cenci's insane but unhypocritical villainy contrasts with the church's hypocritical crimes, Beatrice's genuine goodness is juxtaposed with Orsino's Iagoish postures. And yet Beatrice weighs her goodness, her own just cause, on the dubious moral scale predicated by the church Orsino represents. In Beatrice's first appearance we catch a glimpse of her legalism, a legalism which will provide her with the defense of murder. Her stay against chaos is her complete faith in the moral and religious code. In scene two she hints at this absolutism. She twice rejects Orsino's protestations of love (I.ii.9, 14-15) and swears to "love" him "Holily, / Even as a sister or a spirit might; / And so I swear a cold fidelity." Her devotion to moral right is total, her denial of Orsino fully justified. Nonetheless, however understandable her unwavering piety might be, it unavoidably hardens her. "Ah . . . forgive me; sorrow makes me seem / Sterner than else my nature might have been," she tells Orsino. In her unbearable situation she understandably clings more and more tenaciously to a belief in God and the moral law and so adopts a tragic stoicism which puritanizes her. Such faith is precarious, however just, because it may be converted into a dehumanizing fanaticism. But at this point in the action Shelley stresses Beatrice's sacrificial nature.

Having introduced the antagonists in the first two scenes, Shelley brings them into open contention in the banquet scene which ends Act 1. He underscores Beatrice's isolation from other characters. It is she who first comprehends Cenci's sadistic purpose (I.iii.34), who alone stands against his fiendishness. "[T]here is a God in Heaven" who will not permit Cenci to boast of his sons' deaths, she claims—but God proves no help. She seeks in vain for some defense against the "tyranny and impious hate" of Cenci, but is left to her own resources. Her isolation is crucial to the action. Shelley proposes that until now Beatrice has had two lines of defense: help from outside—the church, Orsino, the people at the feast; and perseverance within—her own all-embracing faith. The first line of defense proves ineffectual, the second ironically effective: the first fails to defend her innocence, the second leads to its destruction. Scene three marks her last desperate attempt to gain outside support and her last legitimate claim of innocence. For a brief moment Beatrice unleashes her potential for revenge when she shouts at Cenci:

> Retire thou, impious man! Ay, hide thyself
> Where never eye can look upon thee more!
> Wouldst thou have honour and obedience
> Who art a torturer? Father, never dream
> Though thou mayst overbear this company,
> But ill must come of ill.—Frown not on me!
> (I.iii.146-51)

Cenci catches something of Beatrice's underlying duplicity, perhaps, when he speaks of her as "Fair and yet terrible!" but Beatrice reasserts her quiet virtue and tells Cenci she will pray for him.

The end of Act 2 seems singularly undramatic. The plot builds toward the rape, but Shelley almost destroys the dramatic effect by adding a fairly lengthy dialogue between Orsino and Giacomo at the end of the act. His intent lies less in plot than character, for it is essential that Beatrice's motivation be fully delineated before Act 3. From a modern dramatist's point of view, Shelley might have found some other means of achieving his end; but we must remember that he was following dramatic convention. Having a secondary character analyze a major one was something Shelley no doubt observed in Elizabethan dramaturgy. In this scene Orsino plays Iago in a closing soliloquy as he analyzes his victim's weakness.

Contemplating Cenci's nature, Orsino ironically foreshadows Beatrice's "pernicious mistake":

> It fortunately serves my close designs
> That 'tis a trick of this same family
> To analyze their own and other minds.
> Such self-anatomy shall teach the will
> Dangerous secrets: for it tempts our powers,
> Knowing what must be thought, and may be done,
> Into the depth of darkest purposes . . . .   (II.ii.107-13)

Beatrice ultimately reaches "the depth of darkest purposes" when she convinces herself by "self-anatomy" that revenge is a just means of defending her purity. Orsino's remarks locate the center of the tragedy within the psyche, and, furthermore, anticipate his deception of Beatrice in Act 3 when he "tempts" her "powers." Shelley here discloses Beatrice's vulnerability to the "black suggestions" of her own mind. The speech therefore provides a necessary transition between the Beatrice victimized by Cenci and the Beatrice victimized by herself.

Glancing backward to the beginning of the act we see a pathetic martyr; looking forward we see an awesome avenger. When she first appears in Act 2, Cenci has already told Beatrice his intent. Her mannerisms forecast her dissolution. In rapid succession she turns for help, first to her brother, then to her stepmother, then to God—"Dost Thou indeed abandon me?" Her speech is choppy, hurried, intense: "He comes; / The door is opening now; I see his face." She visualizes Cenci in direct assault upon her: "He frowns on others, but he smiles on me." Why the rapid disintegration of her spirit? Shelley suggests that only an incestuous rape has the power to break through Beatrice's protective armor and galvanize her into painful self-awareness. When Orsino's servant informs her that "the Holy Father" has refused to consider her petition for help (Orsino never having sent it), Beatrice witnesses the collapse of all sanctioned authority—religion, law, family—and is forced back upon herself. The rape endangers her last source of resistance. Cenci promptly restates his intention to demolish her will:

> from this day and hour
> Never again, I think, with fearless eye,
> And brow superior and unaltered cheek,
> And that lip made for tenderness or scorn,
> Shalt thou strike dumb the meanest of mankind;
> Me least of all. (II.i.115-20)

Cenci could subjugate her body by other means, but only by outrageously transferring his "evil" into Beatrice's character could he require Beatrice to deal with the possibility of her own guilt and shake the citadel of her being.

In sum, the first two acts relate Beatrice's increasingly impossible circumstance and, more importantly, locate the assumptions which empower her to counter Cenci's dynamic attacks upon her will. The locus of the action is within Beatrice, and to see the play in proper perspective we must be sensitive to Shelley's essential concern with the plight of her psyche in a world she can neither control nor abide. The seeming transformation of her character in the "second part" of the play is comprehensible only if we realize that her goodness depends on an erroneous and thus perilous self-definition.

Incest triggers the metamorphosis of Beatrice Cenci. Through rape she enters the world of experience, which according to Blake (as Shelley was aware) leads either to a "higher innocence" or to the Ulro of "rational self-absorption." For Beatrice it leads to both. Until now she has existed in a state of untested innocence, because Cenci has not been able to penetrate the mask of her goodness. Incest, however, makes Beatrice susceptible to the demonic deformity represented by her father. Heretofore, she has fought successfully against the external force of Cenci's evil; hereafter, she falls prey to her own will. The dramatic tension is posited solely in character.

In developing the theme of incest, Shelley inverts popular Gothic tradition. As Masao Miyoshi explains in *The Divided Self*, in Gothic fiction incest is "the supreme expression of social defiance. . . . The incestuous relation, in dissolving the usual familial as well as extrafamilial bonds between individuals, finally dissolves the identifying masks distinguishing one individual from another." Ultimately, he goes on to say, "Given the time-honored sense of the family as an extension of self . . . the incestuous act becomes the moment for the self meeting with itself."[14] In *The Cenci* Beatrice's father does not seek his own independence from the familial bond but, antithetically, insists upon the relationship between Beatrice and himself. In his defiance of all social mores Cenci enacts the most malign of social offenses in order to wipe out the underpinnings of Beatrice's saintly nature. He sets in motion her undeniable need to disclaim the "other self" he unmasks. To exonerate the image he uncovers, Beatrice looks to the moral canon she has accepted completely. Religion, Shelley says in the preface, "is according to the temper of the mind which it inhabits, a passion, a persuasion, an excuse, a refuge; never a check." In the last three acts Beatrice passes through each of the four stages, "proceeding," as Mary Shelley says in her notes, "from vehement struggle, to horror, to deadly resolution, and lastly to the elevated dignity of calm suffering. . . ."

Shelley brilliantly dramatizes the internal nature of Beatrice's plight in the opening speech of Act 3. Beatrice "(. . . *enters staggering, and speaks wildly.*) Reach me that handkerchief!—My brain is hurt. . . ." The reference to "My brain" is totally apt, for the target of Cenci's destructive will is Beatrice's "firm mind," which Lucretia says "Has been our only refuge and defence. . . ." The rape fulfills Cenci's prophecy in Act 2 that Beatrice would "grope through a bewildering mist / Of horror." Now Beatrice laments, "There creeps / A clinging black, contaminating mist about me. . . ." Cenci also predicted that the rape would force her to "confound both night and day," and she observes that "The sunshine on the floor is black."

Stripped of the last vestige of traditional morality, her virginity hideously obliterated, Beatrice insists that the evil exists outside herself but paradoxically demands that it be purged from her own body and spirit. She fears that the rape pollutes "The subtle, pure and innocent spirit of life!" She envisions "contaminating veins" and "putrefying limbs" that "Shut round and sepulchre the panting soul." Something ironic is operating here. Shelley points out in the preface that "no person can be truly dishonoured by the act of another; and the fit return to make to the most enormous injuries is kindness and forbearance, and a resolution to convert the injurer from his dark passion by peace and love." Why should Beatrice feel so threatened? Why should she believe that physical violation can violate the soul? Why should she even ask, "Am I not innocent?"

It seems that, after the rape, the grounds of defense shift dramatically, without Beatrice knowing it, from martyrdom for the cause of moral order to revenge for the sake of self-justification. Shelley suggests that Beatrice's "stubborn will," her self-assured confidence that God preserves the just, is the product of her pride. Beatrice must protect her purity at any cost because she defines herself in terms of an externally applied morality. She can bear any degree of physical agony, but she cannot bear "impurity," "The blot upon my honour"; for to defile her goodness is to invade the innermost part of her being, the stronghold of her strength. Consequently, she wills to expiate "The thing that I have suffered" and to play the avenging God. "[T]o be suddenly convinced of an error," says Coleridge, "is almost like being convicted of a fault."

From this point on Beatrice's "other self," the concealed ego which all along has sustained her, becomes the determinant of action. The passive martyr gives way to the uncompromising judge and executioner, the "Fair" becomes the "terrible." When Orsino enters he finds Beatrice easy prey. She is psychologically susceptible to what the villain Oswald in Wordsworth's *The Borderers* calls "The murdering intellect." Beatrice's "self-anatomy" has convinced her of just cause:

> My tongue should like a knife tear out the secret
> Which cankers my heart's core; ay, lay all bare
> So that my unpolluted fame should be
> With vilest gossips a stale-mouthed story;
> A mock, a byword, an astonishment.   (III.i.56-60)

We begin to suspect that the rape did more to expose than to pollute, that in the "dark caverns" of Beatrice's mind there lurks a gross if unconscious pride. Maintaining self-righteousness becomes her sole object. Therefore Orsino need only imply that God would want them "To punish the crime" in order to entrap Beatrice "in her own loathed will." She concludes, "I have prayed / To God, and I have talked with my own heart, / And have unravelled my entangled will, / And have at length determined what is right." The tyranny which obliterates Beatrice's innocence is not rape but a severe legalism that condemns the judge with the judged.

Beatrice describes her internal state when she locates a likely spot for the murder. The much admired passage is important enough to quote at length:

>   'tis rough and narrow,
> And winds with short turns down the precipice;
> And in its depth there is a mighty rock,
> Which has, from unimaginable years,
> Sustained itself with terror and with toil
> Over a gulf, and with the agony
> With which it clings seems slowly coming down,
> Even as a wretched soul hour after hour,
> Clings to the mass of life; yet clinging, leans;
> And leaning, makes more dark the dread abyss
> In which it fears to fall: beneath this crag
> Huge as despair, as if in weariness,
> The melancholy mountain yawns . . . below,
> You hear but see not an impetuous torrent

Raging among the caverns, and a bridge
Crosses the chasm; and high above there grow,
With intersecting trunks, from crag to crag,
Cedars, and yews, and pines; whose tangled hair
Is matted in one solid roof of shade
By the dark ivy's twine. At noonday here
'Tis twilight, and at sunset blackest night.

                                        (III.i.243-65)

The "wretched soul" is Beatrice, of course, who indeed hangs over the valley of despair. We recognize identifying images. The "tangled hair" refers to the beginning of the scene when Beatrice has first returned after being raped: "How comes this hair undone? / Its wandering strings must be what blind me so, / And yet I tied it fast." The twilight shadows of noonday and the "blackest night" of sunset once more recall Cenci's prophecy that the deed would "confound both night and day" and that Beatrice would "wish for night"—for "the power of blackness." The mountain yawns beneath Beatrice, who, like the rock, "fears to fall" into the abyss.[15] (Given the circumstances, it is difficult to ignore the obvious Freudian overtones in the passage.)

Beatrice reveals herself again when she involves her brother Giacomo in the murder. Shelley has him praise her excessively only to have Beatrice shatter the image he paints. "Let piety to God," she orders him, "Brotherly love, justice and clemency, / And all things that make tender hardest hearts / Make thine hard brother." When he hesitates, Beatrice refuses to hear his doubts—"Answer not." Having asserted her "stubborn will" she casts aside all opposition to it.

In relating the murder in Act 4 Shelley deliberately examines the relationship between Beatrice and her father. He differentiates between Cenci's egomaniacal impulsiveness and Beatrice's perverted egotism. At the same time he substantiates the ironic similarities between the two. Cenci begins the act by reiterating his purpose: ". . . 'tis the stubborn will / Which by its own consent shall stoop as low / As that which drags it down." He tells Lucretia he will perform the worst of terrors, "To bend her to my will" until "She shall become (for what she most abhors / Shall have a fascination to entrap / Her loathing will) to her own conscious self / All she appears to others. . . ." His mission is almost accomplished: Beatrice falls victim to the evil "she most abhors" in her father when she espouses his hate. In a fine dramatic moment Lucretia tells Cenci that Beatrice refuses to come to him, contending that "I see a torrent / Of his own blood raging between us." As if in answer to Beatrice's insistence that the polluted blood separates them, Cenci refers to Beatrice as "this my blood, / This particle of my divided being." He alleges that she is irrevocably his progeny and so a participant in his "evil." If incest divides the self in the conventional Gothic tale, it here operates with a reverse twist. Cenci wills that Beatrice bear a child, a Frankenstein of herself:

> May it be
> A hideous likeness of herself, that as
> From a distorting mirror she may see
> Her image mixed with what she most abhors,
> Smiling upon her from her nursing breast.
> (IV.i.145-49)

Rather than dissolve his relationship with Beatrice, Cenci rivets it by potentially creating a child who is the symbol of their common experience. It is Beatrice who denies "paternity": she flees the other self. The rape forces her to acknowledge that self in the image of the illicit child. Metaphorically, then, the rape holds up a mirror not to nature but to the self, the two faces of Eve magnificently revealed: the pure, the innocent, the long-suffering victim; the demonic, the "unnatural," the hardhearted revenger. In consequence Beatrice becomes more human if less divine, more authentic if less pure.

Shelley draws the parallels between Cenci and Beatrice more boldly as Beatrice directs the murder. Like her father, she fulfills the "dread necessity" with no pangs of conscience. Her charge admits no delay. Just as Cenci threatens those who might help Beatrice at the banquet, she threatens the hired killers Marzio and

Olimpio—"But never dream ye shall outlive him lòng!" Cenci claims that his sleep is "deep and calm," uninterrupted by "conscience"; Beatrice finds herself "strangely undisturbed" after the murder—"I could even sleep / Fearless and calm." Later she sweeps away the prosecutor's arguments at the trial much as Cenci ignores Camillo and his accusers.

But at the same time, Shelley differentiates between Cenci and Beatrice. Count Cenci's involuntary hate is juxtaposed with Beatrice's revenge. He tells Lucretia, "Repentance . . . more depends on God than me." He is little more than the agent of some cosmic force that wills him to abolish Beatrice: "I do not feel as if I were a man, / But like a fiend appointed to chastize / The offenses of some unremembered world." God will not take my soul, he rests assured, "Till the lash / Be broken in its last and deepest wound; / Until its hate be all inflicted." Beatrice, however, is caught " 'Twixt good or evil," compelled by her own will to expunge a blackness within. In murdering Cenci she hopes to eradicate evil when she in fact generates it. After her father's death, she feels liberated:

> Darkness and Hell
> Have swallowed up the vapors they sent forth
> To blacken the sweet light of life. My breath
> Comes, methinks, lighter, and the jellied blood
> Runs freely through my veins.   (IV.iii.40-44)

But in exonerating herself she convicts herself; she confuses self-preservation with justice. As has been pointed out by several critics, Shelley refutes her rationale by the melodramatic device of having Savella arrive coincidentally immediately after the murder with a summons for Cenci to appear in court.[16] The murder it seems was unnecessary and all the more inexcusable.

Mary Shelley thought the fifth act "the finest thing" Shelley ever wrote; but for some critics, the play should end with Cenci's murder. They are surely right—if we conceive of the action in Aristotelian terms as a conflict between externalized forces of good, represented by Beatrice, and evil, represented by Cenci.

We could accept Beatrice's excessive violence as the logical tragic response to Cenci's unmitigated hatred. But Shelley is intent on delineating the full extent of Beatrice's moral decline. The fifth act focuses her duplicity more and more sharply. Throughout the trial scene she alienates us with her incredible coldness; in confronting death she regains our sympathy. Is the problem that Shelley had to rescue her from judgment because he pitied her too much? Did he err in ignoring the logic of the plot, which would demand that the play end with the murder—the tragic conclusion of the struggle between Beatrice and Cenci? Or does the play achieve its ends artistically in terms of the action? If we return to act three we can argue that the play offers its own defense, even if Shelley does impose his sentiment on it. When Beatrice is raped, she foreshadows her revenge, "In this mortal world / There is no vindication and no law / Which can adjudge and execute the doom / Of that through which I suffer." The last act completes her last exasperating attempt to vindicate herself before God and man. Only when she fails in both and exhausts all resources can she gain self-recognition.

The trial is preceded by a short dialogue between Giacomo and Orsino which contrasts the explicit villainy of Orsino with Beatrice's "unnatural" guilt. Moreover, in plotting his own survival in the closing soliloquy, the cowardly prelate illuminates Beatrice's impending fate. He contrives to wrap himself "in a vile disguise" and later to assume "a new life . . . / To change the honours of abandoned Rome. / And these must be the masks of that within. . . ." But he then asks, "where shall I / Find a disguise to hide me from myself . . . ?" He anticipates Beatrice's end. In wearing the mask of innocence during the trial, Beatrice seems totally depraved: she openly lies before the court; she ignores all proof against her; she allows Marzio to be tortured unjustly. Her rationale hinges precariously on her spurious concept of moral justice. Cenci, she debates, "Stabbed with one blow my everlasting soul. . . ." But incest, as Shelley states in the preface, cannot inflict the soul. Beatrice's error lies in her tragic misconception that Cenci marred "my untainted fame; and even that peace / Which sleeps within the core of the heart's heart; / But the wound was not mortal; so my hate / Became the only worship I could lift / To our great father. . . ." Later she asks Marzio, "Think / What 'tis to blot with infamy and blood, / All that which shows like innocence, and is, / Hear me, great God! I swear, most innocent. . . ." More than reputation, fame is the sum and substance of her protection against evil. It is the outer self, the proof of an innocence that if genuine needs no proof. Ironically, in her struggle to retain "fame," the evidence of her virtue, Beatrice embraces a dehumanizing egocentricity as demonic and perverted as her father's.

Beatrice still holds steadfastly to her innocence in a brief scene after the trial. She lashes out at Lucretia and Giacomo because they confess under torture:

> Ha! What was there to confess?
> They must have told some weak and wicked lie
> To flatter their tormentors. Have they said
> That they were guilty? O white innocence,
> That thou shouldst wear the mask of guilt to hide
> Thine awful and serenest countenance
> From those who know thee not!   (V.iii.21-27)

Unable to face the reality of her guilt, she sees them as traitors to her honor. She fears "The vain and senseless crowd," "the light multitude." What memory do you leave us, she asks—"infamy, blood, terror, and despair?" When Lucretia urges her to confess, she chooses the rack. Her fear is not for the body—"My pangs are of the mind, and of the heart, / And of the soul; ay, of the inmost soul." Finding no assurance in earth or in heaven, she approaches the condition Cenci had hoped she would—"Die in despair, blaspheming." Regaining her composure, however, she comforts Lucretia and expresses her conviction that God "Seems, and but seems, to have abandoned us." Finally at the end of the scene she sings Lucretia to sleep. In the song are the words, "There is a snake in thy smile, my dear; / And bitter poison within thy tear." The lines symbolize Beatrice, who although basically good contains within the secret cavern of her mind the "bitter poison" of man's latent demonic nature.[17]

In concluding *The Cenci* Shelley confronted an almost insolvable dilemma. All along he employs a pseudo-Elizabethan plot within which he telescopes the internal drama of Beatrice Cenci. The incest, murder, and trial provide pivots toward which the incidents of plot point. At the same time, Shelley uses these incidents, along with character contrasts and poetic imagery, to project character and thereby translate objective form into subjective matter. But in order to complete the play, he had to abandon traditional dramaturgy. The final change in Beatrice simply could not be handled in a conventional way. The play lacks completion in a classical sense: there is no denouement, no resolution, no reassertion of social law. The societal or cosmic order, on which scale a classical protagonist's fate must ultimately be weighed, is simply irrelevant. If Beatrice were a tragic heroine in a classical sense, her end would affirm the social ethos. Quite the contrary happens. She witnesses the breakdown of all order. The reality she has sought to avoid crashes through the protective wall. At last, when death is imminent and it is apparent that her faith has been misplaced, Beatrice comes to a partial recognition:

What? Oh, where am I? Let me not go mad!
Sweet Heaven, forgive my weak thoughts! If there should be
No God, no Heaven, no Earth in the void world;
The wide, gray, lampless, unpeopled world!
If all things then should be . . . my father's spirit.

(V.iv.56-60)

No longer able to rationalize her actions, she faces the overwhelming question of her existence: "How fearful! to be Nothing!" When Lucretia tells her to "Trust in God's sweet love," Beatrice admits,

your words strike chill:
How tedious, false and cold seem all things. I

Have met with much injustice in this world;
No difference has been made by God or man,
Or any power moulding my wretched lot,
'Twixt good or evil, as regarded me.
I am cut off from the only world I know,
From light, and life, and love, in youth's sweet prime.
You do well telling me to trust in God,
I hope I do trust in Him. In whom else
Can I trust? And yet my heart is cold.   (V.iv.79-89)

She achieves an ironic freedom. Divorced from the cosmic order that she always has assumed existed—her certainty turned to doubt—Beatrice must redefine herself. Disengaged from all else, she is limited to defining herself solely in terms of her subjective consciousness. Says J. Hillis Miller, "When the old system of symbols binding man to God has finally evaporated man finds himself alone and in spiritual poverty. Modern times begin when man confronts his isolation, his separation from everything outside himself."[18] Lucretia's comfort in God's grace is not so much wrong as *non sequitur*. Beatrice's strength no longer lies in what God will do for her, but in what she will do for herself; the categories of being have shifted.

Beatrice gains the intuitive truth that comes from within experience. In consequence the whole of her encounter with Cenci is translated into paradox. The rape becomes a saving rape in that it frees her from a false identity, a parasitic dependence on something outside self. For the romantics knowledge comes about through antithesis. Shelley himself says that the highest aim of drama is to teach "the human heart, through its sympathies and antipathies, the knowledge of itself" (Preface). Count Cenci, like Faust's Mephistopheles, provides a necessary pole in the dialectic, an antithesis which thrusts Beatrice into the world of experience: "Part of a power which would work evil, and ever does good." There is no innocence without its opposite. In cracking Beatrice's outer shell of goodness, Cenci potentially transforms the goodness into something genuine. As with Raskolnikov, Beatrice discovers her encounter to be ironically redemptive.

By her own act she strikes down the mask which conceals the "being within my being."

Beatrice's ultimate but partial defense is that she is human. Because she finds evil in all mankind, in the fabric of life itself, she finds reason to assert her innocence again. In a sense, Beatrice is as innocent as her flawed humanity will allow her to be. Were she, like Prometheus, capable of a divine act of forgiveness, her unwillingness to forgive would be inexcusable. But she is not.[19] Shelley exposes her goodness and guilt at the same time. He highlights the contrast between her psychologically motivated offense and the explicit guilt of the church, as represented in the last act by the judges, the pope, and Orsino. To the end Beatrice acknowledges that "Though wrapped in a strange cloud of crime and shame" she has "lived ever holy and unstained." At the conclusion of the drama we are left with a new kind of protagonist, who unlike the protagonist of old virtually stands outside final judgment. Rather, judgment is not the issue. Shelley neither defends those who condemn Beatrice nor exonerates her of her "pernicious mistake"—the point is, her stoic attitude toward death is existentially earned. She is freed from the prison of her misconceptions and a debunked morality and finds herself alone in an indifferent universe. The end is necessarily irresolute—the cost of freedom is enormous, the victory ambiguous.

Beatrice, then, is not the agent of plot or a metaphoric figure portraying by her actions the inevitable operation of a moral law. In *Hamlet* there exists a cosmic justice which evaluates human action. It is applied from the beginning, and its accuracy is attested by the restored social and political rule at the end of the play. There is no Fortinbras waiting to assume the throne at the end of *The Cenci*, no ritualistic reconciler. Beatrice's own essentially existential experience is the only basis we have of recognizing the validity of any metaphysical law. The inherent paradox of life is not unlike what Strindberg describes in the forward to *Miss Julie*—in this world virtue and vice are somehow "very much alike." Like Beatrice herself, *The Cenci* is a Janus figure looking simultaneously in two directions, backward to a rapidly dissipating metaphysical system and forward to a world of insolvable chaos.

Shelley did not set out to modify dramatic form. His avowed intent was to illumine "some of the most dark and secret caverns of the human heart." To fulfill this he shows how Beatrice is stripped of the "film of familiarity" which will not permit her to pierce the surface of her real being. Some years before writing *The Cenci* Shelley spoke of the "obscure and shadowy . . . caverns of the mind" in an unfinished *Treatise on Morals*. The caverns, he suggests, are "pervaded with a luster, beautifully bright indeed, but shining not beyond their portals." He continues by drawing a distinction between external forces—"the government, the religion, the domestic habits"—which interpose themselves upon a human being and internal forces. "Internally all is conducted otherwise," he goes on to say; "the efficiency, the essence, the vitality derives its color from what is in no wise contributed to from any external source." So in *The Cenci* the action is triggered by the external conflict conveyed by plot, but it resides in character. Cenci's end is foreseen and direct; Beatrice's grows before our eyes as incest activates her subconscious drives. The emergence of her inner self becomes the principle of action. As audience, we watch the circular, mysterious probing of her mind with a growing awareness that the prevailing evil surrounding her emanates from within. This is why the play seems to change focus after the rape and again in the last scene, when experiences illuminate something previously unseen in Beatrice. As her illusions of reality fall, the center of reality moves increasingly inward—knowledge is an act of becoming. The inner conflict in Beatrice—the tough dialectic between two diametrically opposed sets of values, one orthodox and static, one intuitive and dynamic—prefigures the human predicament in a world in which "foul *is* fair, and fair *is* foul."

In the preface to *The Cenci* Shelley speaks of himself as "one whose attention has but newly been awakened to the study of literature." We are tempted to speculate on what might have been had he lived longer and directed his "attention" to the stage as well. But even supposing that Shelley might have acquired a knowledge of stage techniques, he never would have succeeded. Over half-a-century after him, Henry James lamented, "I may have been meant for the Drama—God knows!—but I certainly wasn't meant for the Theatre."[20] Even after Robertson initiated the "new drama" at midcentury and Pinero had begun writing, the English theater had progressed no great distance, in spite of significant modifications and advances in other literary genres. Drama was still incapable of depicting the subtle subjective matter of *The Cenci*. The portrayal of internal reality was still the province of fiction—it remained for Ibsen and Strindberg to show how reality might be internalized or even totally inverted visually on a stage.[21] And Shelley writing for the English stage sixty or seventy years later would likely have remained a potential rather than an actual dramatist.

2

BYRON'S *CAIN* AND *WERNER*

> I come more and more to the conviction that it is not a question
> of new and old forms, but that what matters is that a man
> should write without thinking about forms at all, write because
> it springs freely from his soul.
>
> KONSTATIN TREPLEV in *The Sea Gull*

The Byronic paradox is nowhere more apparent than in the poet's attitude toward the theater. On one hand, he venerated the stage, delighted in seeing his own thinly veiled figure prancing before the curtain, worshipped Kean, idolized Sheridan, respected Alfieri, encouraged the literati to take the stage seriously. On the other hand, he denounced the popular drama, the management, the audience—"the publican *boxers*," "the degradation of our vaunted stage!"—"Oh! motley sight!" Condemning the theater, he served it as a member of the Drury Lane Subcommittee; claiming "aloofness" from the stage, he attempted to reform it. He wrote plays but refused to permit their presentation. Claiming a neoclassic theory, he authored one of the most modern plays in the period; reverencing the classic form, he demonstrated its incompatibility with modern subjective matter. Glancing like Shelley simultaneously to the past and to the future, he ironically pioneered in establishing a modern drama at the expense of the old. So it is, George Steiner concludes, Byron's dramas are "of the first interest to anyone concerned with the idea of tragedy in modern literature."[1]

Byron both courted and was repelled by the stage. As a youth he was interested in acting and the playhouse, but he attacked the popular theater as early as *English Bards and Scotch Reviewers* in 1809 and "Hints from Horace" two years later. With apparent trepidation he assumed the task of writing an address for the reopening of Drury Lane Theatre in 1812. Unable to praise a stage he often derided yet was devoted to saving, Byron tried to reach a compromise between celebration and honesty. When Lord Holland criticized an early draft because of its satiric quality, Byron retorted, "It is impossible not to allude to the degraded state of the Stage, but I have lighted it. . . ." Advising Holland to "cut—add—reject—or destroy" as he would, he sent the manuscript on September 23, only to follow with revisions in letters written on September 25, 26, 27 (two letters), 28 (two letters), 29, 30 (two letters), and October 2.[2] It was an uneasy peace.

Byron's closest familiarity with the stage came about when he was appointed to the Subcommittee of Management of Drury Lane in May of 1815. For a short period of time, he performed his duties with high determination. But if the poet's association with the theater was one of many reasons for Lady Byron's displeasure soon after their marriage in 1815, she could take solace in Byron's inability to find his mistress worthy. He tried in vain to procure decent plays from major literary figures, including Coleridge, whose *Remorse* he had helped stage in 1813. Enthusiasm soon gave way to despair. In hopes of finding something suitable for production, Byron read many of the five-hundred plays on the shelves at Drury Lane. "I do not think," he concluded, "that, of those which I saw, there was one which could be conscientiously tolerated" (*L&J* 5:442). Disgusted by poets who could not write plays, by "the actors, and the authoresses, and the Milliners, and the wild Irishmen, the people from Brighton, from Blackwell, from Chatham, from Cheltenham, from Dublin, from Dundee,—who came in upon me!" (*L&J* 5:442-43),

Byron felt alienated from the stage. He wrote Murray in 1817 that "my intercourse with D[rury] Lane has given me the greatest contempt" (*L&J* 4:55).

As a result of his familiarity with the popular theater, Byron vowed he would never write for production. On April 22, 1815, he went to see Mrs. Wilmot's tragedy *Ina*. The play was bad, the audience worse: "The audience got upon their legs—the damnable pit—and roared, and groaned, and hissed, and whistled. . . . The curtain fell upon unheard actors, and the announcement attempted by Kean for Monday was equally ineffectual" (*L&J* 3:196). To Byron, the experience served as "a good warning not to risk or write tragedies." The "publican *boxers*" and after-dinner-cigar patrons composed an audience Byron refused to please, or feared to test, and he repeatedly insisted that his plays were not to be staged.

But if Byron's association with the English theater is one story, his effort to write drama is quite another. To reject the stage is not necessarily to reject the medium of drama. Although Byron vituperatively damned the theatrical world, he experimented with dramatic form and wrote six complete plays and two dramatic fragments. When he was securely on the continent, disengaged from the Green Room festivities at Drury Lane, the semicomic world of theatrical personalities and the carnival atmosphere of popular performances, he tried to develop a dramatic theory based on neoclassic principles at the same time he ventured toward a new kind of drama. Byron the classicist and Byron the romantic coexist in the poet's dramatic literature as they do in nearly everything he wrote. His dramatic theory and three complete plays, *Sardanapalus*, *The Two Foscari*, and *Marino Faliero*, point in one direction—*Manfred* and *Cain* in another. Abhorring the excesses of the popular drama, which mixed Elizabethan techniques and current Gothic matter to concoct its own brew of melodrama, Byron preached the revival of neoclassic purity and restraint, based on a strict adherence to the unities and simplicity of plot. He prided himself on the tightness of his own plays, boasting that the unity of *Marino Faliero* was "too much observed" to succeed on the English stage (*L&J* 5:81). Of *Sardanapalus*, he said, "Mind the *Unities*, which are my great object of research. I am glad that Gifford likes it: as for 'the Millions,' you see that I have carefully consulted everything but the *taste* of the day for *coup de théâtre*" (*L&J* 5:324-25).

In opposition to the emotional effects and supernatural apparatus of Gothic drama, he sought historical realism in his neoclassic plays. Conscientiously, if indiscriminately, researching historical documents, he repeatedly sent background notes to Murray, his publisher, whenever the plays were being readied for print—"I want to be as near the truth as Drama can be" (*L&J* 5:75). In writing *Sardanapalus*, "I thought of nothing but Asiatic history," he wrote; and *Marino Faliero* "too, is rigidly historical." In sum,

> My object has been to dramatize, like the Greeks (a *modest* phrase!), striking passages of history, as they did of history and mythology. You will find all of this very *unlike* Shakespeare; and so much the better, in one sense, for I look upon him to be the *worst* of models, though the most extraordinary of writers. (*L&J* 5:323)

Responding with admirable caution to the perilous effect of Shakespearean structure on the development of drama, Byron seemed to turn to even more archaic and damning models, the Greeks and, more importantly, the French neoclassicists.

In all major respects, Byron's announced theory was antiromantic. Similarly, his historical plays mirror, in their structure at least, the geometric design of traditional drama. *Manfred* and *Cain*, however, are far less imitative, far more experimental in both form and matter. Byron called *Manfred* a "metaphysical" drama because of its "mysterious," subjective nature. The subjective crisis in the hero dictates the action, but the motivation is not clear. Manfred's "sin" is never made convincing, nor is his remorse. Furthermore, the Gothic machinery which is supposed to serve as an objectification of Manfred's internal turmoil detracts from as much as it illuminates character. As M. K. Joseph has noted, Byron uses "Gothic paradigms for purposes to which they were never adapted." When interest in the narrative is superseded by interest in character, the typical Gothic villain "cannot be made to take too great a weight of introspection and analysis."[3]

Soon after he wrote *Manfred*, Byron half-seriously degraded it as a "piece of phantasy," "a mad Drama," "a Bedlam tragedy," "a 'witch drama.'" He declared his preference for the "classical" drama directly antithetical to it and proceeded to write his "regular" plays. But try though he might, Byron could not hold to the rigidity of the classical pattern in drama. Even in the classical plays soliloquies by major characters contain lengthy lyric passages extending well beyond the demands of plot. After three attempts at traditional drama, Byron returned to what he called his "metaphysical style." He seems to have used the term defensively. He obviously recognized the unconventionality of *Manfred* and *Cain* and seemed particularly anxious to deny them as orthodox dramas. In rejecting not only the stage, which he did in writing the historical plays, but also the very tradition of the drama, by which he justified the "regular" plays, Byron was free to experiment without restrictions in writing *Cain*.

Profiting from his experience in writing his regular plays, Byron avoided many crucial structural faults apparent in *Manfred*. *Cain* is a modern play in defiance of Byron's own theory, yet its success is partly attributable to Byron's experiments with the plotting of classical tragedy. The form is vastly superior to *Manfred*, the matter similar. By using a recognizable Christian myth, Byron saved *Cain* from the obscurity of *Manfred*. Manfred's passionate outpourings could only be presented in strongly emotive language, in vague identifications of inner tension with nature, and in the artificial use of minor characters as reflectors. The autobiographical material in the play further impaired dramatic movement. In *Cain*, however, Byron achieved aesthetic distance by developing a dialectical pattern of action. He was able to objectify subjective conflict through Cain's encounters with other characters. Byron transferred his concern for historical "realism" in the neoclassic plays to "realism" of character. Far more than he himself realized, he created a *"mental theatre."*[4]

In *Cain* we can observe Byron's crucial development toward a new, emerging dramatic form. In the last complete play, *Werner*, we get a clear picture of the typical nineteenth-century stage thriller. In contrast to the highly innovative *Cain*, *Werner* is as derivative and trite as anything Byron wrote in his last years. Conceived and begun in 1815 when Byron was still hoping to be reconciled to the English theater, hurriedly completed in 1821 when he had little to lose by way of reputation, *Werner* is Byron's one play composed for "the Millions." The poet once boasted that *Marino Faliero* was totally unlike the current drama—"nothing *melo*dramatic—no surprises, no starts, nor trap-doors, nor opportunities 'for tossing their heads and kicking their heels'" (*L&J* 5:167). *Werner* is proof enough that Byron understood the popular taste. Viewing it alongside *Cain* gives us a composite picture of both the quiet revolution taking place in dramatic form and the ignominious state of the English stage.

To appreciate the achievement of *Cain* we might begin with *Manfred*. Manfred enters alone in a "gothic Gallery." He speaks his dejection, his Faustian awareness of human limitation and personal remorse. Having commanded the appearance of the spirits of earth and air, he asks of them "Oblivion—self-oblivion." They mock his clay with their immortality. Finally the Seventh Spirit, assuming the shape of the woman Manfred has mysteriously destroyed, entices him to grasp at air. As he "falls senseless" an incantation, spoken by some unseen source, condemns him "Nor to slumber, nor to die," but to "compel Thyself to be thy proper Hell!"

Now picture an altar set against a sunrise in a "land without Paradise." Six characters are already on the stage, the hero perhaps not even distinguishable. This time there is no soliloquy. Rather the play begins with a series of prayers. First Adam, then Eve, then Abel, then Adah, then Zillah pray—"all hail! all hail!" Against these supplications is heard Cain's dissonant reply, "Why should I speak?" The drama has begun.

Manfred seeks self-oblivion to escape the weight of some mysterious act. From the first lines he tells us of his remorse, and he acts under its curse to the end of the play. *Manfred* ends where it begins; the remorse is already present. The sin is so great as to be unmentionable, and the punishment—self-inflicted, subjective torture—becomes the plot. *Cain* does not begin *post facto* but with the cause of remorse; and in fact the action concerns not the expression so much as the cause of suffering. To what degree Byron had transcended the popular Gothic tradition by 1821 is powerfully revealed even in the first lines with the juxtaposition of Cain's solitary, wry retort next to the almost choral hymns of praise that begin the play. By using a Biblical myth as a frame, Byron could objectify conflict at once. In *Manfred* the struggle within is at best indistinct. Unlike Goethe, who made full use of legend to establish an internal dialectic in *Faust* and transform it into a modern dramatic action, Byron failed to exploit the implications of the Faust myth in *Manfred*, even though it is Faustian in matter. In *Cain*, however, he took advantage of one of the greatest myths in Western literature.

Byron called *Cain* " 'A Mystery,' in conformity with the ancient title annexed to drama upon similar subjects, which were styled 'Mysteries, or Moralities' " (Preface).[5] He carefully demonstrated the scriptural basis of the play and justified all additions to the scriptural account. Later he defended it against the charge of "blasphemy" by comparing it to *Paradise Lost*: "I have even avoided introducing the Deity, as in Scripture, (though Milton does, and not very wisely either) . . ." (*L&J* 6:16). In point of fact *Cain* employs Christian myth as a vehicle for the drama of self. Contrary to the scriptural dramas of the Middle Ages, which play upon the audience's familiarity with story to reassert the Scripture's moral validity, *Cain* uses a common myth as a means of conveying a new morality. Without having to create plot or characters (as he unsuccessfully attempted to do in *Manfred*) Byron could communicate directly with his audience. He transposed an internal pattern of action into the well-known narrative, making a "theatre of the mind" out of the Biblical story. Furthermore, he translated the old myth from a paradigm of long-accepted communal belief into the drama of modern man, epistemology giving way to the ontology of self. The representatives of the established moral code, Adam and Abel, were replaced by a villain turned hero, the Biblical plot by the drama of expanded consciousness.

As Act 1 develops it becomes obvious how much Byron had matured in using dramatic form in the four years between the writing of *Manfred* and *Cain*. The use of secondary characters, for example, indicates that he had begun to realize the possibilities of the medium. Cain's first encounter with Adam and Eve is far more realistic than Manfred's conversations with the magical *personae* who haunt him. Furthermore, these secondary characters also function as individuals in *Cain*. They jointly represent orthodoxy, the passive acceptance of life as it is, but each is a distinct character and serves a different need in the action. Adam is cowardly. He questions the God-tyrant—"God! why didst Thou plant the tree of knowledge!"—but unlike Cain shrinks from defiant rebellion. We are prepared for the savagery of Eve's curse on Cain at the conclusion of the play because we discover early in the action that she favors Abel. Abel, of course, is the perfect foil to Cain—orthodox, passive, obedient. Adah is a crucial part of the dialectic which operates in the play: a foil to Lucifer and the symbol of man's transcendent ability to love. In addition, she serves as part of Cain's *raison d'être* after the curse is pronounced on him.

The action also moves more rapidly in *Cain* than in *Manfred*, save for certain portions of Act 2. The soliloquy which begins *Manfred*—conventionally set amid a foreboding Gothic atmosphere of darkness, mountains, and castle ruins—fails to define the reason for remorse, so that the subsequent appearance of the spirits only makes the action more nebulous. But in the first few lines we discover the dramatic situation in *Cain*. The outer conflict is obviously between what the family says about the universe and what Cain's own awareness tells him about cosmic injustice. The quarrel centers on God's reason for planting the tree of

knowledge in the garden and tempting man. Cain insists on probing the reason why the fruit was forbidden. Eve insists that he be
"cheerful and resigned," Abel that he fear to "rouse / The Eternal
anger." When Adah, his wife and sister, approaches, Cain immediately controls his anger. He politely tells Abel and his sister
to go about their labors—"Your gentleness must not be harshly
met." But the brief argument leads him to soliloquize. External
conflict is transferred to Cain's mind: character becomes the locus of the action. And the soliloquy is far different from Manfred's opening monologue. Cain asks a series of questions about
his existence: "Wherefore should I toil?" "What had I done in
this?" Why the tree of knowledge? How do I know that God is
good? The problem Cain faces is intellectual—how can I align
the accepted view of God with my own awareness? The problem
Manfred faces is more emotional and self-restrictive. Manfred
seeks oblivion; Cain seeks understanding. Manfred presents his
inner conflict in impassioned metaphors, in powerful associations
with nature:

> And you, ye crags, upon whose extreme edge
> I stand, and on the torrent's brink beneath
> Behold the tall pines dwindled as to shrubs
> In dizziness of distance; when a leap,
> A stir, a motion, even a breath, could bring
> My breast upon its rocky bosom's bed
> To rest for ever—wherefore do I pause?
>
> (I.ii.13-19)[6]

But because we never clearly understand his motives, the result
is often verbal bombast. Even though the action rises to great
intensity, it is difficult to follow the movement or grasp the meaning.

Cain is placed against a sparse backdrop, "The Land without
Paradise." The altars of sacrifice, symbol of the first family's
obedience to the deity, are the sole stage property Byron describes. The ritual we anticipate in traditional tragedy prefigures
a moral stability existing in nature or the cosmos in general; for

behind the tragic hero, Northrop Frye has written, "there is something on the side opposite the audience compared to which he is small. . . . whatever it is the tragic hero is our mediator with it."[7] Conversely, Byron's hero is heroic because, like Prometheus, he defies the supreme authority a communal drama implies; but unlike Prometheus, and like Beatrice, he is restrained by the limits of his mortality. Cain's Faustian dilemma differs from the Faust legend in that Cain is not a flawed protagonist doomed to pay the consequences of his sin, but, more like Goethe's Faust, an archetype of modern man engaged in an unending search for his identity.

Viewing *Manfred* as a "mad drama" marred by a chaotic plot and obscure language, Byron no doubt was sensitive to the structural needs of his new "metaphysical" drama. How might he externalize a psychological drama of character and still hold to the mythic events? He hit upon the method of using characters to symbolize the poles of the dialectic within Cain. He introduced Lucifer and Adah to furnish the necessary "objective correlative" for Cain's internal debate. Lucifer appears at the proper psychological moment. His first word is electric—"Mortal!" In addressing Cain's humanity, he implies its final definition, death, the consummation of all human knowledge. By Lucifer's appearance on stage, he permits character development in *Cain* that *Manfred* lacks, because *Manfred* contains no means of exposure except Manfred's projections into nature and his own protestations. (The Chamois Hunter and the Abbot hardly possess Manfred's sweeping emotional power.) But Lucifer is capable of competing with Cain and in fact diminishing his pride by exposing his impotence to act in a hostile world. Lucifer supplies a suitable means of visualizing the drama in Cain himself: " 'Tis your immortal part / Which speaks with you." And because he provides a crucial element in the structure as the dialectical pole representing Cain's will to break the bonds of his flesh, he energizes Cain's antithetical impulse to resist the denial of his flesh. In this sense, Lucifer is at once the symbol of Cain's rebellious Promethean nature and a subtle threat to his ability to live a genuine existence within the context of his humanity. The difference between Cain's "clay" and Lucifer's pure spirit gives impetus to the action.

This "posing of polar opposites" results in a more definable conflict than in *Manfred*. In *Manfred* Arimanes is a mysterious spirit representing the woman Manfred has somehow violated. Neither the woman nor the offense is clearly identified. But the flaw Cain senses in the fabric of life generally is clearly the contrast between his humanity and the catalytic superhumanity of Lucifer. Byron himself described the conflict and action of the play:

> Cain is a proud man: if Lucifer promised him kingdoms, etc., it would *elate* him: the object of the Demon is to *depress* him still further in his own estimation than he was before, by showing him infinite things and his own abasement, till he falls into the frame of mind that leads to the Catastrophe, from mere *internal* irritation, *not* premeditation, or envy of *Abel* (which would have made him contemptible), but from the rage and fury against the inadequacy of his state to his conceptions, and which discharges itself rather against Life, and the author of Life, than the mere living. (*L&J* 5:470)

This essential stripping action in the play roughly parallels the two-pronged revelation of self in *The Cenci*. The first step in the unmasking of character is external; an outside force imposes its will and demands on the character: Cenci inflicts incest, Lucifer self-disgust. In both cases, the protagonists are set in opposition to the force, struggling to maintain self-identity in spite of the desire to escape into oblivion. Beatrice tells Lucretia, "O, before worse comes of it, / 'Twere wise to die: it ends in that at last." Cain's nihilism, like Manfred's, is even more intense: he wills never to have been born. Yet Cenci and Lucifer paradoxically thrust Beatrice and Cain toward recognition. The second and more important stripping action, also generated by the antagonists, follows the first: an ambiguous act of will on the part of the protagonist fully exposes the self. Murder in both plays is the final determinant of selfhood. Such self-assertion is tragic: it may lead to the "sickness unto death"; but it is the prerequisite of salvation, the act which frees the self. It saves the hero from total self-annihilation at the same time it fixes his human limitation. As his only act of will—the consummate act of self-knowledge, however ambivalent—murder separates the hero from the community of men and from God. Only a tragic act of will can complete the knowledge of self.

From his first word Lucifer focuses Cain's humanity, and he punctuates the ensuing conversation with addresses to Cain as "poor clay!" But if he derogates Cain, he also inspires him. He informs Cain that he has an immortal part which is manifested in his doubt about God. He entices him to revolt by claiming that God punishes those "who dare use their immortality, / Souls who dare look the omnipotent tyrant in / His everlasting face, and tell him that / His evil is not good!" In praising "Souls who dare" defy "the omnipotent tyrant," he also minimizes God, who "is no happier than / We in our conflict." If God made us, he contends, "he cannot unmake us."

Cain is susceptible to Lucifer's rationale and responds readily to him, just as Beatrice is susceptible to Orsino. He has long seen the gates of Paradise "Guarded by fi'ry-sworded cherubim" and felt "the weight / Of daily toil and constant thought." "I never could / Reconcile what I saw with what I heard," he says; and he gives further reason for his eagerness to accept Lucifer's pronouncements—his alienation:

> My father is
> Tamed down; my mother has forgot the mind
> Which made her thirst for knowledge at the risk
> Of an eternal curse. My brother is
> A watching shepherd boy, who offers up
> The firstlings of the flock to him who bids
> The earth yield nothing to us without sweat:
> My sister Zillah sings an earlier hymn
> Than the birds' matins; and my Adah, my
> Own and beloved, she, too, understands not
> The mind which overwhelms me. Never till
> Now met I aught to sympathize with me.   (I.i.179-90)

Lucifer's concern for Cain is ambiguous, however. On one hand he calls Cain to his fullest potential. "Nothing can / Quench the mind, if the mind will be itself / The centre of surrounding things . . . ," he states. He urges Cain to break anew "The narrow bounds / Of Paradise." When Cain seems to cower at the thought of death and wishes "I ne'er had been / Aught else but dust!" Lucifer scowls at his cowardice, "That is a grov'ling wish, / Less than thy father's, for he wished to know." And this counteraction by Lucifer drives Cain beyond the desire for oblivion and escape from "the unapprehended reality" of the human condition. In a sense, Lucifer is a counterpart of Cain in the spirit world. He shares Cain's rebelliousness and suffers from the same curse. But on the other hand, he represents a distinct threat to Cain's freedom. By subtle manipulation he invites Cain to "fall down and worship me." Offering to substitute one symbol of authority for another, he speaks of "the joy / And power of Knowledge." In refusing to trade one parasitic existence for another, Cain agonizingly, though victoriously, discovers that "knowledge is sorrow."

When Lucifer in the next few lines tempts Cain most fully to "Be taught the mystery of being," however, Cain's only hesitation is his promise to Adah that he would present an offering with Abel. What really stands between Lucifer and Cain is Cain's involvement in the human community, if not his acceptance of social and moral law. Even though he creates sympathy for Lucifer as a rebel against a tyrannical God, Byron no more asks us to identify with him than Goethe asks us to identify with Mephistopheles. Like Cenci, Lucifer serves a fundamentally structural purpose: "as the spirit that always says no" he does not represent belief in rebellion as much as he provides motivation for Cain. By mocking Cain's mortality he compels him to respond. Representing one pole of the internal dialectic, Lucifer stands opposite Adah. The conflict between his negative rationality and Adah's simple human love constitutes Cain's dilemma and propels him toward his own construction of values.

At one pole Lucifer beckons Cain to transcend his clay and worship him; at the other Adah asks a commitment of his flesh. Before Lucifer appeared Cain could only strike out vainly against the sky; now he is empowered to act, to explore fully "the mystery of being." The conflict surfaces when Lucifer engages Adah in conversation and tries to undermine her faith. She does not, in fact cannot, counter his logic; but she makes a distinctly human appeal to Cain: "Cain, walk not with this spirit./ Bear with what we have bourne, and love me. I/Love thee." She reiterates her fear of Lucifer—"He is not of ours." Her only defense against his intellect is her simplistic faith—"Omnipotence / Must be all goodness." She accuses him of tempting "us with our own / Dissatisfied and curious thoughts. . . ." But she also admits that she "cannot answer this immortal thing" or "abhor him." She acknowledges his appeal: "he awes me, and yet draws me near, / Nearer and nearer. Cain, Cain, save me from him!" Adah is latently aware of the injustice Cain openly opposes, an unspoken dissatisfaction with life. Bound to the orthodoxy of belief, she is unable to initiate action, yet she holds desperately to Cain by virtue of her human love.

Lucifer makes the choice intelligible to Cain:

> And if higher knowledge quenches love,
> What must he be you cannot love when known?
> Since the all-knowing cherubim love least,
> The seraphs' love can be but ignorance.
> That they are not compatible, the doom
> Of thy fond parents, for their daring, proves.
> Choose betwixt love and knowledge, since there is
> No other choice. (I.i.432-31)

So Cain is faced with what seems an either-or choice. Adah cries out, "Oh Cain, choose love." He rejects all other love but hers, even the obligation of loving his parents. Adah magnifies her claim by mentioning Enoch, their child. Whereas Shelley uses the "child" to mirror the common "guilt" of Beatrice and Cenci, Byron uses the child to symbolize human love. Enoch's name provokes Cain's horrible prophecy that there will be "unnumbered and innumerable / Multitudes, millions, myriads, which may be, / To inherit agonies accumulated / By ages." Finding in himself the source of future pain—"I must be sire of such things!"—he would be free of the fruit of love as Beatrice would be free of the image of her guilt. Still, he says of his heirs to human woes, "At least they ought to have known all things that are / Of knowledge—and the mystery of death." Adah's final plea is that she must not be left alone—"To me my solitude seems sin. . . ." Each appeal she makes, however, is foiled by Lucifer's sarcasm.

The demand upon self comes first from one side then from the other, until at the end of the act the irreconcilable debate gradually subsides. Adah becomes more pliant, her objections to Lucifer less rigorous, particularly after he compares the "wisdom in the spirit" with the appeal of the morning star to human eyes, an appeal that Adah must acknowledge. "Thou seem'st unhappy," she concludes; "do not make us so, / And I will weep for thee." Significantly, Lucifer responds to her tears—"Alas! those tears" —and identifies in part with her. Finally she asks only that Cain return within an hour from the promised journey with Lucifer. This partial submission to Lucifer on Adah's part gains certain sympathy for him and, most important, permits Byron to proceed to the journey in space without having Cain really decide against Adah's supplications.

Although the expressionistic effects are not developed adequately in the mystical journey through "The Abyss of Space," Byron's intent is to trace the "expansion of consciousness" in dramatic form. He forgoes stage restrictions altogether to record a "mental" drama in Cain. The parallels between Act 2 and the dramatic pattern in Goethe's *Faust* are worth discussing here. Goethe thought Byron silly to follow the three unities in his neoclassic plays, and yet his own "classicism" was every bit as pervasive as Byron's, as his own plays attest. His attempts at traditional form are as contrary to his *Faust* as Byron's neoclassic plays are to his *Cain*. In both modern plays, the authors trace a protagonist's uncertain search for meaning in a spiritually debunked world. Byron's play tends to invert Biblical myth, Goethe's a medieval morality tale. More particularly, action in both plays stems from a conflict, not between good and evil, but between the forces of negation and affirmation within the self, a conflict externalized by Mephistopheles and Lucifer. According to Robert Langbaum, the two voices contending in the plays represent "the difference between eighteenth-century rationalist rebellion which denies the soul and therefore leads to moral destruction, and nineteenth-century romantic rebellion which affirms the soul and therefore leads to moral reconstruction."[8] In isolating Cain as a divided self in dialogue with himself, the journey with Lucifer forfeits the ordinary role of the protagonist as agent of an action and replaces the temporal and causal concerns of plot with thematic and organic unity centered in character.

Lucifer promises to show Cain "the worlds beyond thy little world . . . thy little life." As his imagination and wonder expand, Cain sees the infinitesimal significance of earth and man. Earth becomes "Yon small blue circle," and "As we move / Like sunbeams onward, it grows small and smaller. . . ." As the multitudinous stars "Increase their myriads," earth falls to nothingness. And to the physical shrinking of earth, amid innumerable stars, Lucifer adds the humiliating fact of the "gross and paltry wants" of man to debase Cain all the more. He further insists that all of creation travails under the same curse—"all doomed to death." Cain responds to Lucifer's "prophetic torture" with the death wish—"Here let me die, for to give birth to those / Who can but suffer many years and die / Me thinks is merely propagating death / And multiplying murder." When Lucifer sardonically replies that "Thou canst not / All die; there is what must survive," Cain asks that "What is mortal of me perish." Lucifer answers, "*I* am angelic. Wouldst thou be as I am?" Holding to his flawed humanity, Cain admits, "I know not what thou art. I see thy pow'r. . . ." But he refuses to grant Lucifer spiritual superiority, naming him "inferior still to my desires / And my conceptions."

Ironically, even while Lucifer mocks him, Cain judges him with equal severity. The pace of conversation is slow, yet the action is anything but static. Byron sacrifices plot for character at considerable dramatic cost in parts of the act. Even the verbal conflict is limited, in part because of Lucifer's disinterested tone. Nonetheless, the dialogue implies a subtle tension between the impulse Lucifer articulates and the opposing imperative Cain feels. Although both characters reject the universal order, Cain is suspicious of Lucifer's claims, reluctant to commit himself to one whose "sorrow" is equal to his own. Moreover, his impatience with Lucifer's partial demonstration of knowledge is intensified by a nostalgia for things human. When Lucifer asks if he dares behold "the mysteries of death," Cain accepts the challenge unequivocally: "Clay, spirit! What thou wilt, I can survey." Yet as Lucifer takes him on the descent to Hades, he cries out, "The earth! Where is my earth / Let me look on it, / For I was made of it."

The action points directly toward Cain's knowledge of the ultimate truth about man—Death. In the second scene he descends into that final nothingness of "swimming shadows and enormous shapes." Despairing at Lucifer's degrading revelation of death, he demands, "Cursed be / He who invented life that leads to death!" But his humiliation is still incomplete. Lucifer informs him that the haunted specters of an earlier world which appear before them were once pre-Adamites:

> Living, high,
> Intelligent, good, great, and glorious things,
> As much superior unto all thy sire,
> Adam, could e'er have been in Eden, as
> The sixty-thousandth generation shall be,
> In its dull damp degeneracy, to
> Thee and thy son;—and how weak they are, judge
> By thy own flesh.   (II.ii.67-74)[9]

These were "such noble creatures," Lucifer concludes, and all you share with them is "death: the rest / Of your poor attributes is such as suits / Reptiles engendered out of the subsiding / Slime of a mighty universe. . . ."

Confronted with the absurdity of life, Cain desires to escape self-consciousness, to "dwell in shadows." But at the point of deepest despair when Lucifer bitterly says, "*Their* earth is gone forever . . . Oh, what a beautiful world it *was!*" Cain replies, "And is." Temporarily rejuvenated by recalling the beauty of the physical world, Cain resists Lucifer's profoundly nihilistic vision. Assuming the attack, he tells Lucifer that he still has not provided answers to his questions. When Lucifer counters with the fact that "Thou knowest that there is / A state, and many states beyond thine own, / And this thou knowest not this morn," Cain complains that all still "Seems dim and shadowy." The spirited debate continues until Lucifer draws from Cain the admission that he finds himself "most wicked and unhappy." Cain feels a strange remorse, not because of any guilt or crime, "but for pain / I have felt much." He has sought knowledge in order to achieve "happiness," he tells Lucifer, but finds that knowledge is sorrow and that "my father's God did well / When he prohibited the fatal tree."

Unable to accept either his absurd world or himself, Cain stubbornly clings to his independence. He preserves himself from the "sickness unto death" by counteracting Lucifer's dominant pessimism with Adah's love. When Cain says, "The loveliest thing I know is loveliest nearest," Lucifer can only reply, "Then there must be delusion." Lucifer describes Adah's face as "fair as frail mortality . . . it is delusion." Then he repeats the charged word with which he first greeted Cain, "Mortal, / My brotherhood's with those who have no children." Having to choose between superhuman and human kind, Cain echoes Adah's words, "Then thou canst have no fellowship with us." There is that final separation between the two that Cain cannot bridge, and it is again the image of Adah which prevents him from surrendering to temptation. In spite of all Lucifer's revelations, Cain will not sacrifice his humanity to exchange one kind of servitude for another:

> *Lucifer*: I pity thee who lovest what must perish
> *Cain*: And I thee who lov'st nothing.   (II.ii.337-38)

Once Adah enters into the discussion, the action takes a sharp
turn. To this point we have watched Cain's exposure to the dreadful realities of universal life and his cautious responses to Lucifer's vigorous cynicism. But the reference to Adah destroys the
dominant disinterested view of life which the dialogue with
Lucifer creates. Now Cain's humanity rebels against Lucifer's
debasing vision. At first he asks to see Jehovah's Paradise "or
thine." "[T]hou hast shown me much," he confesses, "But not
all." When Lucifer says that both he and God reign together in
the universe "but our dwellings are asunder," Cain asks why
they came to separate. Lucifer throws the question back to Cain,
"Art thou not Abel's brother?"

>   We are brethren
> And so we shall remain, but were it not so,
> Is spirit like to flesh? Can it fall out,
> Infinity with Immortality?
> Jarring and turning space to misery—
> For what?   (II.ii.383-88)

"To reign," is the reply.
    As Cain reaches for the ultimate truth he speaks with rich
dramatic irony: he will soon slay his brother. But now he dares
"go on aspiring / To the great double myst'ries! the two principles. . . ." He tries to gain the knowledge of good and evil; but
Lucifer again confronts him with his humanity: "Dust! limit thy
ambition, for to see / Either of these, would be for thee to perish."
Cain now exceeds Lucifer's bounds, and when Lucifer admits
that death is merely "The prelude" to another state, Cain recants his earlier desire for oblivion and returns, "Then I dread
it less, / Now that I know it leads to something definite." At
the end of the act, Cain gains a partial victory by refusing to
bow to Lucifer's superiority: "Haughty spirit, / Thou speak'st

it proudly, but thyself, though proud, / Hast a superior." But he is affected by Lucifer's might—"Alas! I seem nothing." As Lucifer defends himself—"I have a victor, true, but no superior"— he identifies with Cain's own mortal part: "And what can quench our immortality, / Or mutual and irrevocable hate?" In writing Lucifer's last words, Byron seems almost to have abandoned him as a character and usurped his voice in order to envision Cain's end. Rather than trying to win his allegiance, Lucifer tells Cain to "form an inner world":

> judge
> Not by words, though of spirits, but the fruits
> Of your existence, such as it must be.
> One good gift has the fatal apple giv'n—
> Your reason; let it not be over-swayed
> By tyrannous threats to force you into faith
> 'Gainst all external sense and inward feeling.
> Think and endure and form an inner world
> In your own bosom, where the outward fails.
>
> (II.ii.456-64)

He urges Cain toward total independence, an independence so great as to destroy Lucifer's own authority. But genuine freedom can be achieved only through Cain's complete knowledge of human existence, a knowledge accessible only through participation in death.

Act 1 reveals Cain's outer conflict with the family of believers and, more significantly, his own subjective crisis. Byron's method is fairly orthodox: he depends on traditional means of exposition and characterization, save for the introduction of Lucifer. In Act 2 he ignores stage conventions in order to place sole emphasis on the internal drama of Lucifer's attack on Cain's spirit and Cain's growing awareness of "the inadequacy of his state to his conceptions." The process of demoralization turns upon Lucifer's ability to inflict Cain with his profound nihilism and so render him impotent to act. His end, like Cenci's, is to undermine the resistance of Cain's will and so gain possession of him. His end is also as ambiguous as Cenci's. In exposing Cain to the spiritual void in the universe, Lucifer places responsibility for constructing a moral order entirely on Cain himself.

Edward Bostetter has contended that "The third act, with its return to the anthropomorphic myth of the first act, becomes dramatically anticlimactical and logically irrelevant."[10] But, as Harold Bloom has noted, in it Cain "completes an act of knowledge."[11] Far from being "logically irrelevant" it is the natural culmination of Cain's realization of his human condition. The first lines of Act 3 magnify the difference between the supernatural and human worlds: "Hush! tread softly, Cain. . . . Our little Enoch sleeps." Cain projects his despair into a description of the innocent boy asleep beneath a "gloomy" cypress. Paradise " 'Tis but a dream," he insists. Adah prophetically asks, "Why wilt thou always mourn for Paradise? / Can we not make another?" But Cain is too deeply immersed in grief:

> I had beheld immemorial works
> Of endless beings, skirred extinguished worlds,
> And gazing on eternity methought
> I had borrowed more by a few drops of ages
> From its immensity, but now I feel
> My littleness again. Well said the spirit
> That I was nothing!   (III.i.63-69)

Again, Adah is the foil. When Cain refuses to accept the "sin" of his parents—"*let them* die!"—Adah replies, "Would I could die for them, so *they* might live!" Cain insists once more upon his innocence and defies God. When Adah charges him with impiety, Cain climactically replies, "Then leave me." Adah's devotion to him passes the final test—"Never, / Though thy God left thee." Rejecting the cosmic order for love of Cain, Adah foreshadows the end of the play.

Set against the emotionally charged conversation with Adah is the encounter with Abel. The psychological moment has arrived for the murder to occur. In anger motivated by his enlarged vision of the loss of Paradise, his awareness of the universality of death, and his debate with Adah, Cain comes upon the prepared altars. He thinks sacrifice "a bribe / To the Creator." His sense of human suffering becomes so profound that he threatens to save his son by dashing him against the rocks. Adah's reply places Cain's identity with the child, just as Cenci attempts to define Beatrice in the image of her potential child, "Touch not the child—my child!—Thy child—oh Cain!" Finally she reiterates her claim upon his love, "Love us, then, my Cain! / And love thyself for our sakes, for we love thee." At this electric moment Abel enters. He comes just when Adah seems to have restrained Cain, but the psychological fact is that Cain has just reaffirmed his love for Adah and Enoch, so that he cannot bear the thought of sacrificing to the God who would destroy them in death. Ironically, the son and Adah partially motivate the murder, for their claims upon Cain are legitimate, whereas Abel's claim upon him as a fellow worshiper is spurious. Abel is persistent in bowing "even to the dust." His prayer is, of course, reverent and somber. Cain's prayer is antithetical to it. He stands unbowed, asking God to receive his offering "If thou must be propitiated with prayers. . . . If thou must be induced with altars / And softened with sacrifice. . . ." Choose my brother's "If thou lov'st blood" or mine if you will accept "an altar without gore." Ironically, he adds,

> And for him who dresseth it,
> He is such as thou mad'st him and seeks nothing
> Which must be won by kneeling. If he's evil
> Strike him. . . . If he be good
> Strike him or spare him as thou wilt, since all
> Rests upon thee; and good and evil seem
> To have no pow'r themselves, save in thy will.
> (III.i.268-75)

When Cain's sacrifice is scattered by a whirlwind, Abel warns him to offer another; but Cain will be no flatterer. Finally Cain strikes Abel with a brand. As he falls, Abel addresses Cain as "brother." Cain echoes, "Brother!" The simple contrast to Lucifer's sarcastic "Mortal!" signals Cain's inescapable humanity. Murder marks Cain's full knowledge of his mortality—he has entered the world of experience. The magnitude of the act is actualized in physical identification, remarkably similar to Beatrice's jarring consciousness of rape:

> This is a vision, else I am become
> The native of another and worse world.
> The earth swims around me. What is this? 'Tis wet,
> (*Puts his hand to his brow, and then looks at it.*)
> And yet there are no dews. 'Tis blood—my blood—
> My brother's and my own and shed by me.   (III.i.342-46)

All along, Cain's defensiveness, his extreme disgust at his human condition, and his unwillingness to accept its limitations or purpose keep him from dealing with his own divided nature. Like Beatrice, he is humanized by the tragic enactment of his pride. And like Shelley, Byron creates a sympathetic hero, nonetheless marred by guilt. The ambiguity lies in the effect of that guilt. For both Beatrice and Cain, the criminal act is a saving act which frees the self from a false pride in the magnitude of self, and yet, paradoxically, leaves the self as the only surviving source of value. Murder, in either case, does not crush the self in order to affirm some law, some definition of being beyond the self. Rather it transforms a fragmented and distorted image of self into something authentic by the catharsis of experience. The awareness of Cain's human commitment is the one act of knowledge Lucifer could not supply. Murder is the knowledge of experience as opposed to reason, a knowledge that marks most fully the separation between the spirit Lucifer and the clay Cain. William Marshall is correct when he writes,

> The life of the mind . . . could not exist for Cain apart from the 'poor clay,' so that, ironically, it must end in the actualization of the Death that has been foretold to Adam: Abel himself must become a sacrifice to Cain's 'clay' rather than to his intellectual principle, to his created imperfection rather than to his Luciferian idealism.[12]

The fact that the murder occurs in the play and is psychologically motivated demonstrates the degree to which Byron learned to use the genre. The implied incest is never admitted in *Manfred*; the "sin" is vividly present in *Cain*, even though it is ambivalent. It is not so much a sin committed by Cain as a manifestation of his flawed humanity. Zillah, whom Abel asks Cain to comfort, exclaims with harsh finality, "Death is in the world!" The word "death" awakens Cain to "the fearful desert of his consciousness." His crime, Leonard Michaels has declared, "is presented so as to make it the justification of an antecedent condition which is subjective and internal." In order to convert myth "to the personal psychology of his hero," Byron makes crime necessary in order for Cain "to identify or account for himself."[13] Murder, the nadir of Cain's experience, gives birth to remorse, the presence of which negates Lucifer's claim that "good" and "evil" are meaningless terms. Remorse verifies the moral values operative in the self.

After Adam, Eve, Zillah, and Adah arrive at the scene, the action moves rapidly. Eve pronounces her savage curse on the first murderer, "May the grass wither from thy feet, the woods/ Deny thee shelter, earth a home, the dust / A grave, the sun his light, and heaven her God!" Although Adah tries to intervene on Cain's behalf, Adam finally disowns him. Cain stands alone, except for Adah; and he tries to force her to leave. At this moment the Angel of the Lord appears. He magnifies Eve's curse by assuring divine protection against Cain's death, disallowing escape of any sort. In a letter to John Murray, Byron claimed to have introduced the Angel "to avoid shocking any feelings on the subject of falling short of what all uninspired men must fall short in, viz., giving an adequate notion of the effect of the presence of Jehovah" (*L&J* 6:16). In choosing to "adopt his Angel" rather than present God on stage, Byron doubtless sought to avoid the attack of conservative critics. By his very harshness God's agent earns our disrespect and polarizes our sympathy for Cain.

When he is marked on the brow, Cain acknowledges a greater internal pain, "It burns / My brow, but naught to that which is within it / Is there more? Let me meet it as I may." He is willing to suffer; and, what is more, he is willing to trade his life for Abel's and consequently attains the transcendent sacrificial love of Adah. As he stares at Abel's body, Cain remarks, "if thou see'st what I am, / I think thou wilt forgive him, whom his God / Can ne'er forgive, nor his own soul. Farewell." He accuses himself not because the Angel of the Lord judges him—such condemnation is irrelevant—but because he has ironically caused "The first grave dug for morality." The act is part of the discovery of truth, according to Stopford Brooke,

> the terror of death is gone when a man awakens to the true meaning of life, whether he wakes to it through being the victor or victim of evil. And better such a waking, however won, even through crime, than the previous dream, for at least we know what we are, and do not imagine that we are only intellect, or only matter.[14]

In causing Abel's death rather than his own, Cain is a new kind of hero. We anticipate the death of the protagonist in traditional tragedy because it makes a public, communal ritual out of the individual's "life." Abel would serve as a more suitable tragic hero, but the curse of continual existence liberates Cain from all pre-formulated ritual, making him the maker rather than the agent of myth, an existential hero.

The action in *Cain* consists of the hero's spiraling rebellion against "the God out there" and his own humanity. At the end of Act 2 Lucifer accuses Cain of wanting to "go aspiring / To the great double myst'ries. . . ." Cain does, but the only way to discover "good" or "evil" is to go beyond the external judgments of the "tyrant God." Ironically, Adam tells Cain early in the play that "evil only was the path / To good." In his prayer to God Cain remarks, "good and evil seem / To have no pow'r themselves save in thy will." In murder Cain fully realizes his own power of evil; and this recognition gives him an autonomy, an understanding which goes beyond the ethical law of good and evil predicated by Adam. In the final sense, murder affirms the rightness of his rebellion against his clay and against the author of life.

Crime leads to the only real moral judgment in a world without moral vitality—the sentencing of self.

The action evolves as Cain moves from sullen passivity to participation. Once he experiences the human tragedy by his own act, Cain goes beyond the stagnant ethical values of his social and moral world. Moreover, he renders Lucifer's subtle temptation void. No Adam and Eve restored to obedience by God's benevolence, Cain and Adah seek a new order—Milton's human archetypes will no longer serve.

Cain is part traditional and part modern. It contains modern, subjective matter within the context of known myth. Unlike Byron's neoclassic dramas, it lays stress on internal movement ("mental theatre") but acquires objectivity through recognized characters and events. Having written in the neoclassic form, Byron knew enough to abandon the poetic excesses of *Manfred*, even while he retained his "metaphysical style." He was able to integrate the new and the old matter. It is revealing that while Samuel Chew offers geometric figures to explain the structure of Byron's plays, he dismisses *Cain* as defying such analysis—"it is so far from regular dramatic form."[15] Baffled by its unusual design, Chew explains the problem as a lack of conflict between good and evil. The lack of architectonic structure more likely stems from Byron's abandoning the simple events of the legend to deal exclusively with the protagonist's struggle to harmonize his Promethean urge toward freedom, catalyzed ambiguously by Lucifer, and his own awareness of his "clay," actualized by the murder of Abel.

Cain comes closer than any play before it in English literature to fitting what Hebbel characterizes in the Preface to *Maria Magdalena* as genuinely modern drama, in which the action resides not in the movement to an Idea but in a dialectical process centered directly in the Idea. In his important essay, Hebbel argues that in Greek drama action is linear, moving directly along a straight line to a moral center, or Idea. Shakespearean drama, with its Protestant ethos, emancipated the individual to a much greater degree, he continues. As a consequence, we see Hamlet constantly interrupt plot by unrestrained introspection. The movement is more a zigzag than a straight line. Goethe later laid the foundation for a truly modern drama in *Faust*, in which he located the dialectic directly in the Idea. The question is not when will the hero reach the moral end, the Idea, but how is he to discover it at all. *Cain's* modernity resides in the rejection of plot as "soul of the action"—the substance of action is the intellectual and emotional intensification of Cain's attempt to construe an order within to replace decadence without.

In one sense, Cain does not change his views at all. Rather his detached intellectual rebellion undergoes the crisis of experience: he commits a "sin" against his own values. The guilt is relative only to him; God's judgment or forgiveness are equally irrelevant. It is not unreasonable to suggest that Byron foreshadows by some seventy years Strindberg's theory that while the naturalist may destroy the idea of guilt, "he cannot wipe out the results of an action." Unable to repent yet unable to escape from his offense, Cain is an archetype of modern man, alienated from God, yet dissatisfied with self. Moving in a wasteland without value or meaning, bearing the almost unbearable weight of self-consciousness, he is the new Adam after which none will come. Morse Peckham suggests that whereas tragedy teaches that man "is inadequate to the conditions life imposes upon us," in a post-Nietzschean drama we visualize a hero who, rejecting all transcendental comfort, confronts the nothingness of his condition. And "in emerging from that nothingness and in encountering it," he creates a beingness—"From that act of creation emerges the sense of value; and the sense of order, the sense of meaning, and the sense of identity are but our instruments for that act."[16] *Cain* anticipates that drama.

In the same year that Byron completed *Cain*, he wrote Hobhouse on 16 October,

> Could you without trouble rummage out from my papers the first (or half) act of a tragedy that I began in 1815, called *Werner*. Make Murray cut out "the German's tale" in Lee's Canterbury tales (the subject of the drama), and send me

both by the post. . . . I am determined to make a struggle for the more regular drama, without encouragement; for Murray and his synod do nothing but throw cold water on what I have done hitherto.[17]

Byron's awareness that his dramas were not popular led him to investigate another avenue to success; he returned to a play begun in 1815, while still struggling on the Drury Lane Committee. He knew what was most successful on the stage; and although he hardly condoned the taste of "the Millions," it is unlikely that he could have begun a play in their presence without being affected by their wants. We know that Byron considered writing plays during the few years before his last departure for Italy. In 1814, he wrote Murray that "Just before I left town, Kemble paid me the compliment of desiring me to write a *tragedy*; I wish I could" (*L&J* 3:16). His fear of the stage probably kept him from the task. Byron was sensitive to criticism and apparently realized that his neoclassic dramas could never gain a readership. The fact that he tried to rework a fragment from an early period suggests that *Werner* was an attempt to gain popularity rather than a serious effort to found a new drama or reestablish an old one. Actually Byron did not even try to follow his neoclassic ("regular") theory but patterned the play after the dictates of the contemporary theater.

Byron remained insistent that his dramas were not for the stage: "I am sorry you think *Werner* even *approaching* to any fitness for the stage, which with my notions upon it, is very far from my present object" (*L&J* 5:31). Yet the play comes much closer to representing nineteenth-century popular drama than any other play Byron wrote. It has been argued that Byron really did want the play presented in spite of his vociferous objections. One thing at least is certain: the play was a success. It had a twenty-five year stage history under the protection of William Macready, who acted the title role to enormous applause. Altogether its popularity lasted fifty-nine years.[18] Byron himself thought the play "good" (*L&J* 6:49). *Werner* was based upon a tale by Harriet Lee called "Kruitzner." When he wrote the Preface, Byron carefully acknowledged his debt and added that it was more the conception than the execution of her story that appealed to him. But the plot of the play is extremely involved and is hardly more than what Robert Escarpit labels it— "une pièce policière."[19] Whether Byron actually intended *Werner* for the stage or not, he did follow conventional dramatic practices.

Werner, formerly Seigendorf, was to have inherited rank and wealth at his father's death, but a "cold and creeping kinsman," Stralenheim, seized the inheritance and for twelve years has pursued Werner. Werner, disguised as a beggar, and in fact qualifying as one, has eluded Stralenheim until now. But through an accident of fate Stralenheim is brought to the distant castle where Werner and his faithful wife, Josephine, are staying by agreement with the greedy Idenstein, keeper of the castle. The lord has just been rescued from the river, whose flooding conveniently seals off the castle. When Stralenheim and his attendants arrive, we learn that Ulric, Werner's long-lost son, and Gabor, a stranger, have saved the grateful Stralenheim from drowning. Werner, in a moment of weakness, steals gold from the newly arrived lord. As a result, his conscience interferes with his joy over his reunion with his son. Meanwhile, Stralenheim suspects who Werner is and sends a messenger to verify his guess. By this time the evidence points to Gabor as the thief, but Werner, struck by Gabor's nobility, hides him in a secret panel. Sometime later, as Werner strolls in the garden late at night, Ulric leaps from the terrace and tells him that Stralenheim has been murdered. Werner concludes that Gabor committed the murder because the secret panel leads to Stralenheim's room. The plot next moves laboriously, if actively, to a climax. Werner regains his rank and wealth. Then Gabor arrives and informs him that Ulric leads a band of banditti and, with Ulric present, tells him that Ulric killed Stralenheim. Once convinced, Werner offers to protect Gabor again and orders him to hide in the tower. It is obvious that Ulric intends to kill Gabor, so Werner goes to the tower to give Gabor jewels and diamonds with which to escape. When Ulric returns to find Gabor gone, he denounces his father's weak remorse and returns to his "foresters," leaving Werner, Josephine and the beautiful Ida, the daughter of Stralenheim, whom he was to marry.

The play consists of melodramatic twists, the artificial manipulation of plot, and Gothic atmosphere. As in *The Cenci* there are eyes which meet: Stralenheim stares but once at Werner and sees through the disguise of twenty years. But the recognition is external; there is no confrontation of souls as there is when Cenci's gaze pierces Beatrice's armor. There is the sensational act of murder; but, unlike Cain's act or Cenci's rape of Beatrice, the deed is more important as a fact in the narrative than as a catalyst of internal action. There is finally a moment of recognition when Werner realizes who the murderer is, but the revelation is more significant as an unraveling of the plot than as an internal moment of truth.

There are possibilities for inner action throughout, but they succumb to the melodramatic external action. Idenstein, for example, whose cynical humor and avarice are obviously a foil to Werner, never really emerges as a character. He provides a surface irony because his total lack of values contrasts pointedly with Werner's basically noble character. Therefore, after Werner steals in a moment of desperation, Idenstein's overt decadence reveals to Werner his own degraded state. But the contrast is never internalized. There are also soliloquies which could be moments of self-introspection, but they serve more as exposition than revelation. When Stralenheim arrives, for example, Werner does not soliloquize about his own desires or reveal his motives; rather he informs us of past details and why he is unfortunately trapped in the castle.

Later, when Werner slips into a secret panel to escape, he says he will "see if still be unexplored the passage / I wot of: it will serve me as a den / Of secrecy for some hours, at the worst." Byron might have used the Gothic setting metaphorically and explored the dark passages in Werner's mind. Certainly by this time Gothic trappings were commonly used for psychological penetration of character. But Byron ignores the opportunity. In Act 3, scene 3, when Werner hides Gabor behind the same secret panel, there is a brief and poorly drawn moment of introspection. Byron makes us think that Gabor is surely the murderer by having Gabor sense a "moral" trap:

> Pray Heaven it lead me
> To nothing that may tempt me!
> . . . .
> . . . Here is a darksome angle—so,
> That's weathered. — Let me pause. — Suppose it
>   leads
> Into some greater danger than that which
> I have escaped. . . .   (III.iii.25-26; 32-35)

But here the soliloquy ends. The internal debate is never realized. The passage is primarily used for suspense, to prepare us for the twist at the end of the play.

Werner, of course, is involved in a moral conflict. He must condemn himself if he is to condemn Ulric, because he himself has stooped to the act of stealing. After his theft he begins to judge himself and repent. But the shift from being a moody sufferer to a repentant sinner is not convincing. He suddenly accepts his guilt, whereas before he insisted on his right to break the moral code: "I must find / Some means of restitution, which would ease / My soul in part . . . ." The apparent motive for his remorse is Stralenheim's death, for which he feels morally responsible. Yet we are asked to accept his remorse without seeing it evolve in Werner. Even when his self-agony reaches a climax at the end of Act 4, there is no clear motivation for the self-struggle. Joseph says that "his discussion on moral responsibility with the Abbot at the end of Act 4 is an attempt to find himself."[20] But if so, the guilt is never defined. He insists on a guilt which he *feels*, in good Gothic fashion. But in terms of a stage, a felt guilt is seldom a convincing guilt, as Byron should have realized after writing *Manfred*. It defies actualization:

> For, as I said, though I be innocent,
> I know not why, a like remorse is on me,
> As if he had fallen by me or mine.   (IV.i.530-32)

It also defies meaning.

And the fifth act is sheer melodrama, completely dependent on the machination of plot. Ulric, Werner discovers, is the real murderer, not Gabor. The plot supersedes character, and so Ulric explains the details of the murder and unravels the mystery of Stralenheim's death, rather than the mystery of his soul. He throws Werner's judgment on him—"common stabber!"—back into his father's face. It is your fault, he asserts; "You kindled first / The torch—*you* showed the path. . . ." Byron could have turned the drama on Werner at this point and exposed the "deepest hell," the recognition of personal responsibility for the offense. But the play ends abruptly with the escape of Gabor and Ulric's desertion of his father. All along we are told about the conflict in Werner; we see neither its motivation nor its end.

In treating a "theological" theme concerned with moral choice and responsibility, Byron might well have turned to his metaphysical style in writing *Werner*. Instead, he chose another course. Contrasted with *Manfred*, and most certainly with *Cain*, *Werner* is a dismal failure. The "moral dilemma" in *Manfred* is lost amid rhetorical flourishes and necromantic absurdities, but it is nonetheless present, evolving, however nebulously, in the very atmosphere of the play. Byron fails in *Manfred* because his form does not conceal his own omnipresence; Manfred, his mask, seems little more than a puppet precariously pacing the dark summits of the Jungfrau. In trying to formulate a structure for action in character, Byron's reach exceeded his grasp. In *Werner*, he ventured no further than the popular melodramas. *Manfred* is a significant failure, *Werner* an insignificant "success."

David Erdman has argued that Byron "rationalized the failure of his plays into a proof of his superiority as a playwright."[21] If so, it is a rationalization well supported. Byron's plays failed to be popular largely because they were unacceptable to the age, unacceptable because they looked either backward to a form past resurrecting or forward to a form not yet born. Sitting with three of Byron's plays before him, the practical Lord Jeffrey looked rather at his own age and asked a totally logical question:

If Lord Byron really does not wish to impregnate his elaborate scenes with the living spirit of the drama—if he had no
hankering after stage-effect—if he is not haunted with the
visible presentment of the persons he has created—if, in
setting down a vehement invective, he does not fancy the
tone in which Mr. Kean would deliver it, and anticipate the
long applause of the pit, then he may be sure that neither his
feelings nor his genius are in unison with the stage at all.
Why, then, should he affect the form, without the power of
tragedy?[22]

Why indeed? If Byron did not write for the stage, then for what?
"I have a notion that, if understood," he wrote Murray, the plays
"will in time find favour (though not on the stage) with the
reader." Erdman points to Byron's "purpose" with justifiable
suspicion, and yet the fact is that Byron only once tried to accommodate the current stage in his crusade to reform English drama.
No romantic tried more *not* to succeed on the stage while simultaneously maintaining interest in dramatic form. Byron must
have known beyond any question that *Cain* could never have
been produced in his age; still, he wrote the play as a play.

In cancelling out production as a motive, Byron predicted stage
history. George Steiner has written that "if Byron's plays are
failures, they nevertheless contain within them preliminaries to
some of the most radical aspects of modern drama."[23] If *Cain's*
journey into the Abyss of Space and into Hades seemed impossible on the nineteenth-century stage, *Peer Gynt* could make a
similar one half a century later. If *Cain's* metaphysical import
shocked and repelled almost every contemporary reviewer, a
much greater irreverence was soon to develop in naturalistic
drama. If the metaphysical plays were condemned for their subjective matter, Strindberg was to make psychological drama an
artistic fact. If Byron half conceived of a "mental theatre," Pirandello long after depicted the search for "inner essence" in his
relativistic "cerebral drama."

John Drinkwater expressed the hope in 1925 that Byron's plays
might be presented on the stage.[24] He had in mind the neoclassic
plays. Since then, it is apparent that *Cain* is the most suitable

play for our own age, as a successful production at the University of Chicago in 1968 attests. In the effort to adapt classical myth to a modern sense of reality, *Cain* has a close affinity with a current literature devoted to that end. Irving Babbitt once decreed, "The lack of inner form in so much modern drama and art in general can be traced to the original unsoundness of the break with pseudo-classic formalism."[25] Byron's dramas show that it was a break born of necessity. Trying to restrict his lyrical, subjective impulse to a classical structure, he experienced, Robert Escarpit has noted, "en même temps pour la forme dramatique attraction et répulsion."[26] Embarrassed by the failure of *Manfred*, he turned to history as subject and applied the unities, only to find it impossible to marry his romantic ego to eighteenth-century formalism. Owing to the themes and characters already familiar in the narrative, Byron hit upon a solution in the mythic account of the first murder.

Using the elements of legend, he inverted the myth, unwittingly demonstrating the differences between what Robert Brustein has called "the theatre of communion" and "the theatre of revolt":

> By the theatre of communion, I mean the theatre of the past, dominated by Sophocles, Shakespeare, and Racine, where traditional myths were enacted before an audience of believers against the backdrop of a shifting but still coherent universe. By theatre of revolt, I mean the theatre of the great insurgent modern dramatists, where myths of rebellion are enacted before a dwindling number of spectators in flux of vacancy, bafflement, and accident.[27]

Action in *Oedipus Rex* takes place at the palace of the king, the symbol of social order, and the presentation itself at the temple of the gods, symbol of cosmic order. The communal oneness is played out in the ritualistic pattern of the myth. The climax of *Cain* occurs at the altars, one of which is now chaotically strewn about. This time there is no ritual, no submission to the gods, no return to equilibrium. Cain's offering makes a mockery of ritual. Ostracized by a "sin" he accepts distinctly as his own, separated from a God he does not wish to obey, he is in the largest sense still in the community of men, although separated from the society of men. He walks East of Eden to become himself the maker of a new myth. Modern drama, it might be said, is myth in the act of being born.

3

TENNYSON'S *MAUD* AND *BECKET*

> It is small wonder that the enigma of human consciousness
> with its conflicting intuitions should from the outset appear as
> a dominant motif in his poetry.
>
> E. D. H. JOHNSON, *The Alien Vision*

As though embarrassed at giving birth to a play at age sixty-five
and yet determined to show it could be done, Tennyson looked
upon a theater defiled by "sensational curtains," "brainless pan-
tomime," and "gilt gauds" and dared to risk production. His labor
is the last illustration of a major nineteenth-century poet's attempt to bring life to an Elizabethan stage form long since held
in disrepute. His child was stillborn, the too human product of
a marriage between ancient form and modern matter. He was no
Abraham; he had no miracle.

No other poet might have been expected to have done more
to advance English drama. Writing at the end of the century,
Tennyson could have profited by the failures of his predecessors
to found a modern drama. No contemporary maintained interest
in the stage so long as Tennyson; few were more familiar with
stage personalities. No one had more opportunity to work with
a stage or enjoyed more encouragement from its patrons than this
poet laureate of some twenty-five years standing. Above all, no
one had proved himself so adventuresome and far-reaching in in-

novating modern poetic forms. Short subjective pieces like "The Two Voices" and "Tithonus," the experimental dramatic monologues, the painfully introverted elegy *In Memoriam*, the radically transformed romance epic *Idylls of the King*, the "monodrama" *Maud*, all point toward a modern preoccupation with internal reality. And yet facing a drama ripe for change in an age of intense experimentation on the Continent—Hugo, Hebbel, and Zola already having called for a new kind of drama, Ibsen already having written six plays—Tennyson futilely tried to revive the past. Why?

No one answer will suffice. It could be that Tennyson was too sympathetic with the popular stage, too conditioned by familiarity with it to observe it with a critical eye. It could be that he was guilty of Shakespearean idolatry, like many other poets. It also could be that he prostituted himself too completely to entertain the masses, or gave himself too freely to his stage mentor Henry Irving, or wrote his plays too late in his career. Something of truth lies in all of these explanations, but the most important answer is that Tennyson simply could not envision how dramatic form might be employed to portray the kind of modern subjective action centered in his best poems. He had solved the structural difficulties of projecting the unity and coherence of subjective action in poetry by abandoning continuous narrative form in favor of the broken associational patterns of *In Memoriam* and *The Idylls* and so foreshadowed a symbolist poetry built upon "a complicated association of ideas represented by a medley of metaphors . . . to communicate unique personal feelings."[1] When he wrote for the stage, however, he did not have the same freedom to innovate, the same exciting experimental modes to follow that he inherited from the romantic poets. His choice of Shakespeare as a structural model was almost as inevitable as Shelley's similar choice in writing *The Cenci* over a half-century earlier. The "monodrama" *Maud* and the historical drama *Becket* show that whereas Tennyson had a sense of modern subjective action in character, he could not escape the deadly influence of traditional dramatic form when he wrote for the stage.

Maud is not a traditional narrative poem because, like *In Me-*

moriam, it is a fragmented montage of thinly related symbolistic projections of character rather than a continuous external action. It is not a drama because there is no attempt to make public via a stage the private action in character. But if *Maud* sheds little light on the effort of nineteenth-century poets to write actable plays, it provides irrefutable testimony that Tennyson could conceive of dramatic action in a modern sense. To discuss its method is to define a new kind of associational poetry that old generic labels do not fit. It is one of the most complex and innovative poems of the century and is of consequence to this study because its dramatic movement, if not its form, suggests the outlines of a new drama.

There are several reasons for viewing *Maud* as a drama. In later editions Tennyson called *Maud* a monodrama, and as such it has an affinity with several other nineteenth-century "monologues of feeling" which have a dramatic intent but focus exclusively on one character—Byron's *Manfred*, Arnold's *Empedocles on Etna*, the dramatic monologues of Browning to mention a few. His interest is in character and inner action, rather than in plot. Just as he dramatically modified narrative forms to produce a poetic structure suited to his purpose in *In Memoriam* and *Idylls of the King*, so he rejected standard models for *Maud*. Apparently, Tennyson considered *Maud* an experimental poem, but he also envisioned it as a dramatic action. We gain insight into Tennyson's dramatic intent in his well-known reference to *Maud* as "slightly akin to 'Hamlet.' " What he admired most in *Hamlet*, according to his letters, was the way Shakespeare depicted Hamlet as caught between madness and sanity. He praised Henry Irving's interpretation of *Hamlet* because he felt the acting "showed the 'method in his madness as well as the madness in his method.' "[2] In other words, Tennyson interpreted *Hamlet* primarily in the manner of nineteenth-century criticism as a study of character in which action is basically internal. It is also significant that he first subtitled *Maud* "A Madness," suggesting that his interest was in describing the circuitous evolution of a partially deranged consciousness through "different phases of passion."[3]

The result is a kind of stream of consciousness structure emerging from a *dramatis persona*, the sole center of action. The lover's absolute autonomy means that there is no significance outside the character himself. Plot is not the structural determinant in relation to which a classic protagonist might serve as agent. It is rather, like everything else in the poem, a means of charting the internal movement emanating from the speaker's frustrated consciousness in "fragments of evocation."[4]

The three parts of *Maud* may be summarized briefly as follows: Part 1 describes the hero's despair over his desolate state; his gradually developing love for Maud, which temporarily lifts him out of his "lonely Hell"; the opposition of Maud's brother, who wants her to marry a "new-made lord"; and the garden scene, in which the hero kills the brother in a duel. Part 2 is a somber monologue in which the hero reflects on the deed and its consequences. Part 3 is a statement of his decision to enter the Crimean War. Because the dramatic locus of the poem is the hypersensitive mind of the fictional "I," the external incidents are not important for what they do to the speaker but what they reveal of him. The external action is effect, not cause, and evolves in conjunction with the internal developments.

Throughout, the narrator totters precariously in a state of psychic imbalance. Denied all human association, tortured by the memory of his dead mother and the constant vision of his father's body "Mangled, and flatten'd, and crush'd, and dinted into the ground,"[5] he suffers the great disease of modern man: the inability to act. Like King Arthur in the *Idylls*, like the "I" of *In Memoriam*, he lives in a world stripped of all values. The whole objective world dissolves into a grotesque pattern of horror: the "lips" of the hollow "are dabbled with blood-red heath," and "The red-ribb'd ledges drip with a silent horror of blood." Nature is "tooth and claw," and society is ruled by "the spirit of Cain." Even the Hall his family once owned is occupied by "that old man" who "left us flaccid and drain'd." In one way the speaker's problem is the same as Faust's and the same as Hamlet's (interpreted in light of Victorian criticism): the total collapse of the outer world has rendered him impotent. Yet he is more modern than either Hamlet or Faust in the almost totally hopeless ineffectuality of his condition. He lacks their heroic stature, and his psychological weakness is far more pronounced.

The action is the record of his agonizing search for some sense of identity, some reason for existing in a world alien to his being. The whole of nature is described according to his distraught vision. Scenes and events never assume values of their own, but rather expose the half-crazed speaker, who in projecting his ever-changing moods transmogrifies setting into an image of self. Consequently, the movement is fragmentary, a montage of dissonant sights and sounds. The speaker moves from discussing violence in nature to expressing his contempt for the new lord of the Hall, to the universal evils in the world, as one idea seems to lead to another with only vague association. The vacillating "phases of passion," depicted in the poem by the marvelously inventive control of sound and imagery, form a series of barely related passages.[6] The action moves disjointedly and discursively from the speaker's initial despair to his renewed hope that Maud might save him from his world and himself. The hope diminishes when he fears "She may bring a curse," and he seeks almost total self-negation: "I will bury myself in myself, and the Devil may pipe to his own." Countering the narrator's ineffectual existence, Maud offers an alternative which he is psychologically unable to accept; and yet he is paradoxically drawn to her.

The would-be lover frees himself from all association—"And most of all would I flee from the cruel madness of love"—and yet he cannot bear the "passionless peace" of separation. He blames his condition on the gross materialism of his age, on Maud's father and brother, on the harshness of nature, which he finds, like the narrator in *In Memoriam,* in violent conflict:

> The Mayflower is torn by the swallow, the sparrow
>   spear'd by the shrike,
> And the whole little wood where I sit is a world
>   of plunder and prey.   (I. IV. iv)

But the chaos is internal. His psychological disequilibrium, caused in part by the frenzied suicide of his half-sane father and loss of his mother "who was so gentle and good," has rendered him incapable of action. Nonetheless, even while his inability to face reality results in his emotional railings against the universe at large, it also results in his compensatory need to create some ideal force of love with which he can identify without risking himself. Half aware of his psychic imbalance, he awakens briefly to his condition: "What! am I raging alone as my father raged in his mood?" Seeing himself as the potential victim of his father's fate, he addresses himself:

> Would there be some sorrow for me? There was love in
>   the passionate shriek,
> Love for the silent thing that had made false haste to the
>   grave—
> Wrapt in a cloak, as I saw him, and thought he would
>   rise and speak
> And rave at the lie and the liar, ah God, as he used to rave.
>   (I. I. xv)

Alienated from a father turned traitor, "the silent thing that made false haste to the grave," and a mother idealized in his mind, he first chooses to escape the world ("Be mine a philosopher's life in the quiet woodland ways"); but the need to be loved is more potent than the desire for solitude. Fearful of love yet desirous of it, he makes Maud a symbol of love. He is unable to accept her as a physical lover, conceiving of her subconsciously as a substitute for his mother, but he reaches out to her as Idea ("a precious stone," descendant of "snow-limb'd Eve," "a pearl," "Queen rose," "Queen lily") in passages of exotic ecstasy. She becomes the replacement for that which he has lost, a mechanical goddess concocted to redeem his loveless state: "Ah Maud, you milkwhite fawn, you are all unmeet for a wife. / Your mother is mute in her grave as her image in marble above . . . You have but fed on the roses and lain in the lilies of life."

When he "overcomes" his fear of "the new strong wine of

love" and the "coquettish deceit" which Maud, "Cleopatra-like," may weave, he falls into fits of complete emotional abandon (the great lyrics of the poem). He envisions himself in a private paradise, secure from the evils of Maud's brother and the world he fears. Rather than becoming the means of his renewed association with mankind, Maud becomes a part of the speaker's isolation from the world and a manifestation of his divided self. His condemnation of his own father and his sympathetic identification with his "long-suffering" mother, whose "shrill-edged shriek . . . divided the shuddering night" and yet rings in his psyche, is now assimilated in his distorted assumption that Maud is somehow free of her father's and brother's "guilt." He fabricates the total offense of her brother ("that huge scapegoat of the race"), rejecting Maud's insistence that he is "rough but kind" and that he "left his wine and horses and play" to tend Maud "like a nurse" when "she lay / Sick once." Significantly he associates Maud only with her mother and insists that she is "nothing akin" to her father. In other words, he fashions her to satisfy his psychological need for "someone to love me" and simultaneously projects his own father's "guilt" into her brother and father. The action moves unpredictably from somber, meditative passages to frenzied excitement, as the lover thinks he has "clim'd nearer out of lonely Hell."

In order to possess the "pearl" who is "a counter-charm of space and hollow sky," the speaker translates Maud's image from something threatening ("Faultily faultless, icily regular, splendidly null"—"cold and clear-cut"—"Dead perfection") into an idol of worship (a "rose," "a dove with the tender lip"). At one point he recalls seeing her in church where "An Angel watching an urn / Wept over her." Her pride has vanished, he supposes; in reality she has never changed; rather he has been aroused by a growing passion. In an incredibly ironic passage, he vents his "jealous dread" of the rival "new-made lord" Maud's brother wishes her to marry ("a waxen face, / A rabbit mouth that is ever agape"):

> I wish I could hear again
> The chivalrous battle-song
> That she warbled alone in her joy!
> I might persuade myself then
> She could not do to herself this great wrong,
> To take a wanton dissolute boy
> For a man and leader of men.   (I. X. iv)

The "wanton dissolute boy" is unmistakably ambiguous. Superficially it refers to the "padded shape" who is asking Maud's
brother for her hand, but it also refers to the speaker himself. He
unwittingly ends his speech with a suggestive lament: "And ah
for a man to rise in me, / That the man I am may cease to be!"
In the very section in question he sorrows over the death of his
mother like a lost orphan. He desperately reaches out for "one
to love me"; and returning to a recurring theme, he adds, "What
matters if I go mad, / I shall have had my day."

The lover continues to make Maud's brother the antithesis of
her goodness. Offended by his "barbarous opulence," he tells
Maud he sought to "give him the grasp of fellowship," only to
receive in return "a stony British stare." As always, we have only
the speaker's word that the brother is unapproachable. (Earlier the
speaker admitted that *he* kept "aloof" from the brother.) Moving
skillfully by subtle associational patterns, the monologue on the
brother's arrogance provides a mental transition into the lover's
consideration of Maud's father. Although he has seen the father
only once, he assuredly labels him "a gray old wolf." He convinces himself that Maud cannot belong to her father: "She
might by a true descent be untrue." Again, he once more relates
her to her mother's "sweeter blood." The brother alone has assumed "the whole inherited sin," he surmises. Finally, alluding
to the mother as "a thing complete, literally disconnected from
the father and brother," to Maud as only her child, he exposes
his own divided nature. Psychologically motivated, he invents a
situation mirroring his "private war": Maud's father-brother
takes on the guise of antagonist blocking his pathetic attempt to
repossess in Maud a "mother's love."

Maud, however, cannot resolve his inner conflict. In fact, she is a demonstration of it, not a cure. In total selfishness the lover claims her on the grounds that "Maud's dark father and mine . . . / Betrothed us over their wine, / On the day when Maud was born." He grasps at Maud as a child grabs a toy ("Mine, mine— our fathers have sworn") and wants to flee with her to his private paradise. He has been lifted from a subjective Hell by love; but, ironically, the love is born of his disintegrating mental state. He still cannot live in the real world; he only ignores it ("what care I"). The action crescendos as we come to the end of Part 1 of the poem. Psycho-sexual connotations appear in the speaker's description of a rivulet linking the lover's "empty house . . . half-hid in the gleaming wood" with the Hall where Maud now lives. Coming to meet Maud in a rose garden symbolic of the Garden of Eden, the lover is so emotionally intoxicated and introverted that the whole external world becomes a phantasm: the flowers dance to the music in the Hall and the lily and rose become the audience to his thoughts. Sexual overtones abound ("And the soul of the rose went into my blood") as the entire passage breaks into ecstasy.

The ensuing duel with the brother is also a symbolic revelation of the internal action. The lover's psychic disequilibrium, already demonstrated by the contradictions, exaggerations, and inchoate direction of his thoughts in the previous sections, makes him highly vulnerable to the least provocation. His unstable condition, like a taut spring able to uncoil into extreme elation or absolute despair, incites him to impulsive revenge. It is clear that Tennyson is concerned here with the internal action in character only. By restructuring the extraneous details surrounding the event according to the narrator's impetuous reenactment, he virtually disregards them. The duel is relevant only as an extension of the speaker's mind—"murder" is the incident that generates the ultimate subjective crisis in the poem. When he kills the brother, the speaker consummates his passion for the "ideal" Maud of his own fanciful design. Having destroyed the illusion, he more than ever retreats into himself. The "blood" of the morning dispels his spurious paradise: "O dawn of Eden bright over earth and sky, / The fires of hell brake out of thy rising sun."

Having created the conflicting forces of illusion and reality operating in the lover's consciousness, Tennyson drops the narrative in order to achieve full dramatic impact, preferring to fill in the details of the episode by means of the speaker's reflections in the next part of the poem. Any further development in the narrative at this point would have been impossible given the mental condition of the teller. In dropping the account of the duel just at the point of greatest tension, Tennyson remains true to his structural concept. The issue is not what the character does but what he is, not what those other than the lover might do to redeem the killing, but what the lover might do to redeem the self.

The scene suddenly skips to the French coast where the lover escapes reprisal for killing Maud's brother. As the lover reenacts the duel in his mind, Tennyson creates a masterful alternating rhyme scheme to convey the undulating psychic movement. According to Ralph Rader, "the duel and its aftermath may be thought of most fruitfully . . . as Tennyson's symbolic acting out of his aggressions which he had felt toward those who had helped to thwart his love of Rosa [Baring] and Emily [Sellwood]."[7] But we need not regard the poet's life in order to recognize the contextual significance of the duel to the fictional "I": it is a symbolic incest. The key lies in the complex relationships among the characters. The scene brings together the various figures, both actual and imaginary, who haunt the hero's mind. Just as he has come to view his own parents as polar opposites, so he sees Maud's mother and father. In the garden scene, Maud's father is represented by the brother ("scapegoat of the race"), her mother by Maud herself. They in turn embody the narrator's perverse view of his own traitorous father and idealized mother. The internal dialectic created in the lover's mind is negated by Maud's unwillingness to reject her brother. The speaker recalls that at the conclusion of the duel Maud uttered "a passionate cry, / A cry for her brother's blood" (a reenactment of his mother's "shriek" at his father's death). In killing the brother, the lover ironically reveals Maud's indelible relationship with him. Both literally and symbolically, her blood and her brother's are the same. When the agitated hero kills one, he slays the other as well (in Part 2 Maud is assumed dead). In terms of the internal action the sword becomes a sexual symbol, the "murder" an act of incest. In destroying his antagonist, the lover assaults Maud, the replacement for his mother's love. The meaning is implied when the narrator remembers seeing a ring on the fallen brother's hand "and thought / It is his mother's hair."

The garden scene is a dramatic reversal: for the first time the lover acknowledges the brother's "goodness" (" 'The fault was mine,' he whispered, 'fly!' ") and accepts his own guilt—"The fault was mine, the fault was mine." The illusory Maud is irrevocably annihilated and the hero turns into himself, hoping that "some kind heart will come / To bury me, bury me / Deeper, ever so deeper." Once the false image of Maud is obliterated by his own hand and so also his unnatural attraction to her, the lover might discover another, more authentic "Maud." The "rose" at the end of the poem (ostensibly the Crimean War) is potentially that new "Maud," no longer the object of a "private war" but a public deed. At this point, however, the "I" is inflicted with the "sickness unto death," unable to live on any terms with himself or the world of men.

Stunned into a perilous impassivity, sitting upon a hillside restlessly "Plucking the harmless wildflowers on the hill," the lover is haunted by a "ghastly Wraith" that casts him into a subjective purgatory. He wills to flee not only from others but from himself, from his own self-awareness. Driven to an uncompromised recognition of his guilt, confronted by the "mechanic ghost" of Maud, he desires oblivion, a state of nonbeing. When he could claim to be Maud's lover, he could see himself as superior to the manifest world of evil around him. Maud filled a psychic need for self-justification. With the illusion dissolved by his own deed, he is forced to witness his impotency and guilt. The sickened hero says of Maud, "She is but dead," and of himself, "the time is at hand / When thou shalt more than die." He tries to escape into a dreamworld where he might "find the arms of my true love / Round me once again!" but the dream is turned into a nightmare by the "shadow" which imposes on his private world. His "wakeful doze" is shattered by "that abiding phantom cold" ("thou deathlike type of pain") that represents the full measure of his deranged, depraved condition: " 'Tis the blot upon the brain / That *will* show itself without." His imagined Garden of Eden is replaced by the cruel, inverted image of the city, where "The day comes, a dull red ball / Wrapt in drifts of lurid smoke / On the misty river tide." The marketplace is no more accommodating or sympathetic than the "Red-ribb'd hollow behind the wood." His alienation is deeper than ever, and what was before self-imposed exile is now a complete inability to exist in the human community: "And I loathe the streets and squares / And the faces that one meets, / Hearts with no love for me." Too weak to bear the punishment inflicted by his own conscience, still selfishly looking for someone to love him, destitute of courage to act, he longs "to creep / Into some still cavern deep, / There to weep, and weep, and weep / My whole soul out to thee." Ultimately he undergoes figurative burial in a "shallow grave . . . / Only a yard beneath the street," where dead men pass "up and down and to and fro" over his body "And the wheels go over my head."

With the lover's morose hope "To bury me, bury me / Deeper, ever so little deeper," the action seems frozen in chaotic indirection. Totally introverted, incapable of rationality, the speaker reaches the point of madness—moving from maudlin self-pity to bitter denunciation of the "Wretchedest age since time began," from fear of Maud (now "a juggle born of the brain") to utter detestation of the self, from dreams of the idyllic garden to the reality of a living grave. At this point Tennyson faced a tremendous problem: how could he resolve the action when the hero is left all but "wholly dumb" in the tangled web of his consciousness? How could he rescue him from himself? Tennyson closed off all possibilities of resurrecting him by traditional means because no sense of a communal myth in which a classical protagonist participates is operational in the poem. Unlike Hamlet, the

"I" cannot transcend his own psychological and moral problems by fulfilling a ritualistic role. All along Tennyson places the action in his narrator's overwrought psyche rather than in an arrangement of incidents directed toward a given end. In one sense, the fact that the action is exclusively in character negates the possibility of a completed drama at all, in that the "I" has already proven conclusively his erratic and uncertain nature. Consequently the solution has to be partial and in fact ambiguous, impinging as it does on the inadequate ability of the hero to cope with the loss of identity rather than on a mythic pattern in which he plays an assigned part.

War serves Tennyson's purpose. On one hand, by attaching himself to a new cause, the hero is able to free himself, if only temporarily, from his psychological hell. The war is important to the action only in that it provides an alternative to his passive self-pity.[8] In going to war he achieves a partial reintegration and, for a while at least, is "one with my kind." On the other hand, the decision cannot permanently resolve his problem because it permits him to act without reconciling the differences between the inner and outer worlds. The war does not synthesize and integrate the two worlds; it only permits the hero an impermanent "stay against chaos." Not knowledge, but participation is important. In a traditional action, war would be an end; but, as Robert Langbaum has written, "drama, in the old sense of a completed action, becomes impossible where we do not bring an effective ethos to the poem."[9] War is a means of self-assertion in a dramatic action without a foreseeable end. Like every other incident in the work it marks a phase of development in character, underscoring rather than betraying the associational ordering which constitutes action in the poem. Like Faust, the hero is viable so long as he can escape from the nothingness which leads to inaction or death. The drama can end only when he succumbs to the forces of negation; it continues so long as he engages in an action. Part 3 is not a martial hymn to the Crimean War: the deed may be public, the meaning is private. The great sin is the conclusive sin against self: death, or inaction, the nadir into which the hero falls in Part 2.

To summarize, *Maud* is important to this study because it demonstrates that Tennyson had a sense of modern action in character. It is a "mental drama" in which characters (the "evil" brother, the "new-made lord," the "Queen rose" Maud, the "dark" father, the "gentle" mother) exist only as chimeras in the consciousness of an unpredictable, morose narrator. These are characters without communal dress (no kings, princes, or archbishops), more related than not to the nebulous shapes which haunt *A Dream Play* or *The Ghost Sonata*. Even if *Maud* is not a play it is strikingly similar to Büchner's iconoclastic drama *Woyzeck* in its delineation of a human being deteriorating within from the force of the consummate destroyer, the self. To be sure, *Maud* employs techniques of poetry rather than many ingredients of drama. Yet Tennyson describes setting as the hero projects himself into it with rich variations and "unrealistic" qualities much as a modern expressionistic dramatist might conceive it on a stage of expressionistic design, luminous colors, and interpretive lighting. In writing a poem as opposed to a play, Tennyson uses lyric forms to convey a dialogue of the mind as he had done in earlier poems like "The Two Voices." But his concept of a monodrama limited to one character is not impossible to envision on a modern stage. Arthur Miller's *After the Fall*, for example, is similar in that it demands the presence of the central character for the entire length of the play and presents other characters as embodiments of past experiences and possible choices which flash before his mind.

If Tennyson had had our modern stage to write for with its "elements of personal idiosyncrasy as against drama based firmly, like religious plays, on communal cults or beliefs,"[10] he might have written *Maud* as a play. To have adapted *Maud* for the English theater of the 1850s, however, he would have had to create an entirely different action and exclude the very matter which modern expressionistic drama presents: a grotesque external world depicting an internal distortion in character. The fact that Tennyson did not try or even conceive of the possibility of staging *Maud*, even though he compared it to *Hamlet* and referred to it as a "monodrama," suggests that he did not consider the stage the proper medium to express his concept of internalized, subjective action. Consequently he used poetic form, and, even here, discovered that traditional modes were not suited to his purpose. He wrestled with the difficult problem of fusing dramatic and lyric matter into a single poetic form and invented a new narrative-dramatic structure, his monodrama. Dramatic matter in poetry is different from drama in a theater, however. What Tennyson was able to describe in his poetry he could not transfer to a stage; he could not escape the drama of the past.

Tennyson's familiarity with the drama dates back to the training he received from his father at Somersby. When he was about fourteen years old, he wrote a clever blank verse comedy called *The Devil and the Lady.* He did not quite finish the Jonsonian-type play, and it was, in fact, not until a half-century later that he returned to drama as an art form. In the MS books of 1833-1840 he scribbled out the rough outline of a scenario for a musical masque concerning the Arthurian legends, but the work was not realized (*Memoir* 2:124-25). Nevertheless, Tennyson never lost interest in the theater or disassociated himself from the stage. Sir Hallam Tennyson describes his father's active support of the theater during his middle years, particularly from 1846 to 1850, when he "enjoyed 'turning in' at the theaters" with his friends: the Kembles, Coventry Patmore, Frederick Pollock, Alfred Wigan, and William Charles Macready (*Memoir* 1:268). He greatly admired Macready and wrote a sonnet in his honor when the actor-manager retired from the stage:

> Farewell, Macready, since to-night we part;
>   Full handed thunders often have confessed
>   Thy power, well used to move the public breast.
> We thank thee with our voice, and from the heart.
> Farewell, Macready, since this night we part,
>   Go, take thine honours home; rank with the best,
>   Garrick and statlier Kemble, and the rest,
> Who made a nation purer thro' their art.
> Thine is it that our drama did not die,
>   Nor flicker down to brainless pantomime,

And those gilt gauds men-children swarm to see.
Farewell Macready; moral, grave, sublime;
Our Shakespeare's bland and universal eye
Dwells pleased, thro' twice a hundred years, on thee.

If, as the sonnet suggests, Tennyson knew the contemporary stage, he detested its all too common bill of fare. Some years later he rebelled against the contrary excesses of the new "realism" and romantic "unreality." He condemned the "sensational curtains" which aimed at artificial effects and felt that the stage too frequently confused "the theatric" with "the dramatic" (*Memoir* 2:174-75). He knew the playwrights of the forties, and he knew the pioneers of a more modern drama: Gilbert, Robertson, Tom Taylor.[11] The stage itself was undergoing a minor revolution around the time Tennyson was named poet laureate. The Covent Garden–Drury Lane monopoly was finally abolished in 1843, and by the time Tennyson wrote for the stage at least forty playhouses were active in London. Tom Robertson and the Bancrofts ushered in a new concept of stage management. Restraint in acting replaced the declamatory breast-beating style of the earlier period. Actors, managers, and even playwrights could earn living wages. Stage lighting, costumes, and scenery became more realistic. Social drama, largely under the influence of Robertson, countered the fading popularity of romantic melodramas. In this period of flux and excitement Tennyson decided somewhat apprehensively to write for the stage. Unfortunately, he made two fatal mistakes: he chose to follow a dead dramatic tradition and he wrote for the wrong manager.

Paull Baum touches on one of the key factors resulting in Tennyson's failure as a dramatist—"the English stage in the eighteen seventies offered no sound literary tradition for drama, no proper models." Consequently, Tennyson "fell in with the nineteenth-century tradition of closet drama . . . the Elizabethan tradition modified by literary rather than theatrical considerations."[12] Tennyson failed because he ignored the modest advances of the stage of his day and because he copied some of the worst aspects of the earlier nineteenth-century dramas. Like Shelley, Wordsworth, Coleridge, and Byron, he did not familiarize himself with stage requirements. But to these general faults can be added another consideration which kept him from developing a modern drama: he attempted to write plays about England in a way which eclipsed action in character with historical matter. Social and political material obscured individual internal conflicts. Generally speaking, Tennyson copied some of the worst aspects of works like Browning's *Strafford* with few of the achievements.

The trilogy, *Queen Mary* (1875), *Harold* (1877), and *Becket* (1879), portrays "the Making of England." Tennyson researched books and historical documents faithfully in preparation for writing the plays, even more so than Byron researched his neoclassic dramas. He wanted to examine the contributions of each of the main characters by revealing their personal conflicts and victories, but the very nature of his historical perspective negated the possibility of any real treatment of character. Unknowingly, Tennyson created his own artistic dilemma. *Queen Mary*, for example, has forty-five speaking parts, not to mention minor characters who appear throughout, such as lords, officers, pages, and "others." In the five acts of the play there are twenty-four scenes, so that the stage is in constant flux. *Harold*, Paull Baum notes, is obscured by four separate plots: the nationalistic drama of England's destiny; the "tragedy of the fatal feuds of the two ruling houses"; the tragedy of Harold himself; the drama of intrigue.[13] In addition, there are excessive asides and an abundance of entrances and exits (fifteen in the first act alone). *Becket* is also clouded by the use of broad stage effects and multifarious plotting. What might have been a study of character in the modern sense is instead more a comprehensive historical study modeled on nineteenth-century versions of Elizabethan drama. Although it comes closer than the other two plays to being good drama, its encompassing range diminishes the significance of Becket's role as a character in conflict with himself, in spite of Tennyson's desire that Becket be the focal point of the action.

The four plays which followed were also semi-historical studies. In the use of foreign, mysterious settings (Galatia and

Renaissance Italy) and the melodramatic plotting, the two short plays *The Cup* (1881) and *The Falcon* (1879) follow the popular nineteenth-century tradition. *The Promise of May* (1892) is set in the English countryside and deals with farmers rather than the aristocracy. In an experimental vein, Tennyson abandoned poetry when he first wrote it and then rewrote it in verse "for the reading public"; but except for the semirealistic use of prose dialect, *The Promise of May* is a fairly typical domestic "tragedy." *The Foresters* (1892) is little more than a sentimental melodrama about Robin Hood and Maid Marian. In short, the plays reflect more Tennyson's effort to copy a dead drama than to found a new.

Tennyson committed a second unwise choice in addition to following a dying dramatic tradition: he chose Sir Henry Irving as his manager. James P. McCormick has written that "when Macready failed as actor-manager in 1843 there was literally no theater for serious original plays until the Bancrofts opened at the Prince of Wales's in 1865 and helped create the new Robertsonian drama."[14] The "new drama" certainly had a chance to develop by the time Tennyson began to write for the stage in the 1870s. But the advances still had not gone far enough for a serious writer to imagine the construction of a drama given over to a whole new concept of reality. Most of the improvements were in stage technique and stage realism. And even if the stage had provided the incentive for Tennyson to experiment with dramatic form, it is unlikely that he would have established a new drama. He was sixty-five years old when he first wrote for the stage and could hardly have acquired an adequate knowledge of stage technique at that point in his career. At any rate, by looking to Irving to produce his dramas, Tennyson committed himself to a prescribed structure.

Irving was energetic and successful. In 1878 he took command of the Lyceum, where he had been acting for over a decade. As George Rowell notes, he believed in theater as art and sought "artistic unity" in his productions. He used gas lighting with great effect and was responsible for many technical advances.

But "Irving the actor clearly made little use of the restraint practised by the Bancrofts and their disciples."[15] If he looked forward to a new stage in his many technical innovations, he looked back in other, more crucial, ways. He returned to earlier melodramas, the French "well-made" play, the excesses of the early nineteenth-century romantic drama. When in his last years a new realistic drama emerged, Irving harkened back to Sardou, and, as a result, suffered the hostile criticism of critics like the young Bernard Shaw. He turned away from the Robertsonian drama and was diametrically opposed to Ibsen, "whose plays would have afforded no scope whatever for his particular gift of theatrical illusion." A Shakespeare idolater, Irving took a half-Aristotelian, half-romantic approach to drama, as indicated by his lecture on "The Delineation of Characters in Drama." He admired Kean for his blend of "the Realistic with the Ideal" in acting, and he once advised a group of would-be actors, "An actor should learn that he is a figure in a picture." "All art is mimetic . . . ," he believed; and an actor "can not only help in the illusion of the general effect, but he himself can suggest a running commentary on what is spoken."[16]

When Tennyson gave Irving free rein to alter his plays, the inevitable happened. Tennyson wrote *Queen Mary* "in the hope that some actor or dramatist might think it worth while to edit the play for the stage." When Irving took up the challenge, he cut out more than half of it in order somehow to make it fit for the stage. Undoubtedly Tennyson wrote *Becket* with Irving in mind. The acting manager first thought the play completely unworkable, even though he was predictably attracted by its "picturesque possibilities," especially "the picturesque aspect of the struggle between Court and Church."[17] It is revealing that Irving asked Tennyson to adapt the mawkish narrative poem *Enoch Arden* for the stage instead. Irving later revised *Becket*, cutting out many of the more lengthy speeches inclined toward the subtle portrayal of character. He viewed *Becket* as "a true 'miracle' play —a holy theme"; he viewed its hero as an archetypal "saint." Irving's colleague Bram Stoker informs us that the great actor "was turned to sacerdotalism; and the robes of a churchman sat easy on him." Whether or not Tennyson thought Becket a character self-defined in the action or a classic hero reenacting the biography of a saint, Irving knew all too well that Becket "was cleric before all things."[18] The result was a play in the Irving tradition: episodic in its structure, given to "illusion" and spectacle, but touched with moments of "passion and pathos" profuse enough to show off Irving's considerable acting skills. The original *Becket* is not a plausible stage play; only Irving's hand could make it so. Nor is it a modern drama. Irving's alterations simply made this more apparent.

Becket is representative of Tennyson's uncertain concept of dramatic form. Undoubtedly his concern with historical authenticity accounts for much of the bulkiness and diffusion of the play. By his own admission, his major intention in the historical trilogy was to "pourtray the Making of England"; but he wished to do so by examining the lives of three national heroes. His purpose was necessarily divided—on one hand he wanted to emphasize character, on the other hand a historical plot. From one point of view Becket seems an agent in the action, a legendary figure acting out his part in the destiny of England, rather than the creator of action as was the speaker in *Maud*. Tennyson seems to have seen no parallel between the *Idylls of the King* and *Becket* as historical studies. In the *Idylls* he dealt with basically nonfactual mythic matter and was free to concentrate on character as imaginative creation. In writing *Becket* he felt bound by historical detail. Characters in the *Idylls* undergo subjective crises which motivate their actions, whereas Becket plays out a predetermined role. The first work involves Tennyson's perplexing endeavor to create modern myth, the second his effort to produce representational art. In addition, Tennyson wrote *Becket* for Irving, whose stage and style of acting were more suited to producing plays of panoramic scope, intense stage actions, and grand gestures than plays dependent on subtle, subjective characterization.

On the other hand, there is reason to believe that Tennyson

saw *Becket* as something other than an Elizabethan chronicle play. For one thing, the title suggests an interest in character as much as in history. By placing emphasis on Becket rather than on Henry, the symbol of the social order, Tennyson indicated his interest in exploring the psychological implications of Becket's willing martyrdom. According to his son, Tennyson unquestionably thought *Becket* an investigation of character:

> My father's view of Becket was as follows: Becket was a really great and impulsive man, with a firm sense of duty, and, when he renounced the world, looked upon himself as the head of that Church which was the people's "tower of strength, their bulwark against throne and baronage." This idea so far wrought in his dominant nature as to betray him into many rash acts; and later he lost himself in the idea. His enthusiasm reached a spiritual ecstasy which carries the historian along with it; and his humanity and abiding tenderness for the poor, the weak and the unprotected, heightens the impression so much as to make the poet feel passionately the wronged Rosamund's reverential devotion for him . . . when she kneels praying over his body in Canterbury Cathedral.
>
> (*Memoir* 2:195)

If Tennyson sensed aright that the true drama lay in Becket's gradually aligning his "dominant nature" to a self-affirmed martyrdom, a process evolving from indefinite rashness to total identification "in the idea," why could he not bring it off within the context of dramatic form as he had done so brilliantly with similar actions in the novel poetic forms of earlier works?

In fact the play does contain instances in which Tennyson tries to expose Becket's inner conflicts, but these passages are lost in the inchoate movement of the external action: plot consistently overrides character. The inclusive sweep of the play engulfs Becket in a display of historical figures and events. There are twenty-five speaking parts, not including knights, monks, beggars, "etc." Furthermore, Tennyson includes accounts of involved political maneuverings gleaned or inferred from historical documents. The intrigue of the play becomes a primary structural device, as Becket is involved in a struggle not only with Henry but also with Queen Eleanor. All of the manipulation of scenes necessary to keep the two major plots going (Henry against Becket, Henry and Becket against Eleanor) leaves little opportunity to probe the internal action in character. Nonetheless, the drama is distinguished by its degree of psychological realism. A synopsis will indicate the structural impasse imposed by Tennyson's divided interest in plot and character.

The prologue establishes the rhythm of the play. Probably borrowing from the opening scene in *A Woman Killed with Kindness* and especially Middleton's *A Game at Chess*, Tennyson begins the play with Henry and Becket at chess. He uses the game for expressly the same purpose as his predecessors, to establish intrigue:

> *Becket*: Why—there then, for you see my bishop
> Hath brought your king to a standstill.
> You are beaten.
> *Henry*: (*Kicks over the board*). Why, there, then—
> down go bishop and king together.
> I loathe being beaten. . . .

The function of the incident is to foreshadow the collision of the two men.

The subplot is also presented in the prologue, and here again Tennyson follows an Elizabethan convention. Becket is forced to protect the king's mistress, Rosamund. When Henry shows Becket the hideout where Rosamund will stay when he is abroad, Becket notices the "blood-red" line which marks the way to "Her Bower." The impending catastrophe implied by the blood image is enlarged by various actions which fuse the two plots. For example, when Henry offers to make Becket archbishop, he "lays his hand on Becket's shoulder." But Becket withdraws, calling his arm "A soldier's, not a spiritual arm." The inner conflict in Becket between physical and spiritual strength is actually what Tennyson thought to be the essential action in the play, but this subjective conflict is diminished by Becket's involvement in the external plotting. Just when Becket begins to evaluate his deficiency as a spiritual leader and so begins to probe his own character, Tennyson compounds the plot with the untimely entrance of the queen and her ruthless knight, Fitzurse.

Ostensibly, the queen serves two purposes. First she deepens the intrigue by her all too obvious insights:

> Becket! O,—ay—and these chessman on the floor—
> the king's crown broken! Becket hath beaten thee
> again—and thou hast kicked down the board. I
> know thee of old.

Aware that Henry has a mistress, she complains against "this poor world . . . that is no better ordered" and drives the king "a-hawking." She focuses the subplot and muddies the central conflict between Becket and Henry and consequently the conflict within Becket himself. Because Becket is only peripherally engaged in the clash between the king and queen, he is relegated to a minor role in one of the two major plots of the play, in spite of Tennyson's intention to emphasize his hero's ultimate choice of martyrdom. Eleanor also serves a second function in the scene: she elevates Becket as a character by praising his ability as a soldier and statesman, but she warns that he is not a churchman. In this way she supposedly illuminates the basic struggle in Becket between his temporal and spiritual strength, a duplicity which Tennyson fails to exploit effectively in the ensuing act. Before the first act begins, Becket is embroiled in a complicated situation from which he can never really extricate himself in order to achieve independence as a character.

Act 1 is garbled simply by stage commotion. There are forty entrances and exits within this long, four-scene act. The opening scene between Becket and his friend Herbert is intended to depict the subjective action in Becket, his divided devotion to the king and to the church; but the dialogue is too much dominated by foreshadowings of plot, not introspection. Becket predicts accurately that the chancellor's and archbishop's robes together are "more than mortal man can bear." But just when the self-conflict unfolds, Rosamund enters disguised, "flying from Sir Reginald Fitzurse." From this point on, physical conflict governs the action. She tells Becket that Fitzurse once "sued my hand" and with his evil friends (De Tracy and De Brito) once tried to assault her. Becket's choice soon becomes merely how he must fight the forces of evil, as soldier or priest. The possibility of self-analysis is thereby minimized by the events. The next scene perpetuates the stage movement by suddenly shifting to a street fight between Eleanor's and Becket's retainers.

The fight supposedly objectifies the hidden conflict between the Machiavellian queen and Becket, the agent of the king. Ironically, Eleanor implies which choice Becket must make between church and king, but she gives the wrong reason: "That Church must scorn herself whose fearful priest / Sits winking at the license of the king." According to Tennyson Becket must align himself with the church not primarily because of the king's affair with Rosamund but because he is called by destiny to redeem a depraved society. At this crucial point, Tennyson might have engaged Becket in dialogue with himself in order to bring him to self-recognition. Instead he introduces yet another encounter, this time at Northampton Castle. Here as elsewhere he seems caught between giving full attention to character and furthering the plot. Knowing only a long-established drama of plot and writing with one eye toward production on Irving's stage, he invariably sacrifices character.

The scene at Northampton apparently demonstrates that Becket is not yet worthy of his calling. He weakens enough to sign "and swear to obey the customs" set up by Henry to control the church. The arguments used to persuade him to obey the king's decree are similar to those used by Eliot's four tempters in *Murder in the Cathedral*: physical threats, the king's honor, "The secret whisper of the Holy Father," the assurance "thou wilt hear no more o' the customs." Becket signs impulsively, without any self-introspection; the arguments seem extraneous to character. Just as quickly he recants and refuses to seal the document. When Becket is isolated from all external support, including that of the church ("If Rome be feeble, then should I be firm"), there is every reason for Tennyson to depict internal turmoil in his hero. For one brief moment Becket realizes that he has been "False to my-self—it is the will of God / To break me, prove me nothing of myself!" Turning from both "Henry's gold" and from Rome "venal ev'n to rottenness," he is unable to act. He tells Herbert in despair, "I will suspend myself from all functions." But the king rushes in and the scene ends in verbal conflict. Becket leaves and returns later dramatically "holding his cross of silver before." As quickly as the indecision in character rises to the surface it is submerged; and Becket can tell his would-be successor Foliot, "I, bearing this great ensign, make it clear / Under what prince I fight." The act of deciding is therefore subordinate to the deci-sion itself. And so the scene ends with the new archbishop's anger with the barons—"Mannerless traitors." The contest be-tween soldier and priest within Becket is reduced to the level of his halfheartedly controlling an urge to assault his enemies. That he should fight is no longer the question; nor does his rejection of Henry cost him internal agony. Tennyson had to choose: he could not sustain interest in plot and at the same time freeze the plot in order to reveal the drama of Becket's choice—he opted for plot.

The last scene illustrates the problem once again. Becket's re-tainers leave him in fear of the king, and then the "earls and barons" boycott his banquet. Subsequently he brings in the poor off the street to eat the food. When the knights demand to know where the archbishop is, the beggars refuse to tell them and praise Becket as defender of the poor—"Vive le Roy! That's the English of it." By using the scene to venerate Becket, Tennyson all but eliminates any chance of getting inside his hero. Since Becket is clearly confirmed an English hero by those other than himself, he is freed from justifying himself to himself. All that remains is for him to act out his ritualistic role.

The next three acts, which together are no longer than the first act, mostly are set in Rosamund's bower, where the restricted set-ting afforded Tennyson various opportunities to concentrate on dramatic action in a single character in ways impossible in the expansive court scenes. He does try to focus inner action in Henry. As Rosamund picks a briar-rose and tells how she loves such roses "More than the garden flowers," Henry mutters a confession of his "foul" sexual appetite which makes him unworthy of the innocent Rosamund. Rosamund is unaware that he is married and does not hear his admission that he and Eleanor "have but one bond, her hate of Becket." The emphasis of the scene, however, does not fall on the king's subjective crisis so much as on the obvious parallels between Eleanor and Rosamund: both are referred to as flowers ("rose" and "violet," "wildflower" and "garden-flower"); both have borne Henry a child; both are married (one legally, one spiritually). There is no complexity in their characters: one is clearly evil, one innocent. And the troubled conscience of the king, which might have been examined further, is no longer exposed. Then too, Becket's relationship to the whole affair is indirect. He is supposed to protect Rosamund, but at the same time he cannot, as archbishop, approve of the illicit affair. Actually, the scenes at the bower are not much concerned with Becket; their basic function is to further the plot by having Henry give Rosamund a small crucifix Eleanor had given to him. The use of such an object to set up the unraveling of the plot is a device commonly used in the "well-made" plays and mimics a long established convention in drama. Tennyson hints that the cross is a veiled ironic reference to Becket, but he makes little use of it as a symbolic device.

The second scene introduces yet another character, Walter Map, a malcontent modeled on that Elizabethan stage type. Irving cut out this character because he cluttered an already overcrowded stage, but Tennyson employs Map as a semicomic means of measuring his hero. Map magnifies Becket's problem by sarcastically attacking his allegiance to the church and urging union with the king. Above all, he creates a new enemy for Becket: "Rome, Rome, Rome." Tennyson, Protestant that he was, apparently felt it necessary not to make a Roman Catholic saint of Becket. The reference to Rome serves little purpose in the plot however, and Irving, in this respect, was wise to delete the scene. More importantly, Tennyson not only obscures the plot; he fails to take full advantage of the opportunity of getting into Becket as a character cut off from everything outside self. Rather than rejecting the institution of the church as motive for his acts and so finding his only authentic justification within himself, Becket announces only that his allegiance is not to the Rome of "avarice" and "craft."

Meanwhile Rosamund discovers that Henry is married. As she begins to encounter herself—

> I am in the dark,
> I have lived, poor bird, from cage to cage, and know
> Nothing but him—happy to know no more,
> So that he loved me—

the scene is interrupted. Her child averts "some dreadful truth . . . breaking on me," and the scene ends abruptly. The last two scenes repeat the pattern, save for a slight glimmer of internal action when Map tries to win Becket to Henry's side. At virtually every point where subjective action is possible, Tennyson feels compelled to return to the machination of plot. And yet he builds these passages to emotional peaks. The pattern suggests that while he was interested in internal action he did not know how to describe it or felt it could not be primary in importance on a stage. He keeps up the pace of stage action with a never-ending parade of scenes and characters, entrances and exits.

The whole of Act 4 is devoted to Eleanor's attempt to murder Rosamund and her child in the "dark inland wood." Becket appears only briefly near the end of the act when he conveniently grabs Eleanor's hand "from behind" as she is about to strike Rosamund. It is the weakest act in the play. The gimmicky use of the cross which Eleanor now finds around Rosamund's neck, the heroine's excessive goodness and loyalty, the melodramatic entrance of the archbishop at the point of high suspense are all characteristics of the third-rate melodramas of the period, so also is the end of the act when Becket sends Rosamund to a nunnery and Eleanor swears to have Henry "Against his priest beyond all hellebore."

It is revealing that probably the most effective psychological passage in the play concerns Henry rather than Becket (the other most effective scene, Act 3, scene one, deals with Henry and Rosamund). Tennyson is forced to manipulate too many characters. Given the number of actors in his play and his reluctance to employ old-fashioned soliloquies to isolate characters for purposes of self-analysis, Tennyson simply could not consistently single out the development of any one character. In the scene in question, Act 5, scene one, Roger of York swears allegiance to Henry. He has crowned the young prince and expects, therefore, that his enemy Becket will be removed. The Bishop of Salisbury also hopes for Becket's downfall. And Henry, who has always loved Becket, insists, "I have lost all love for him." At the right psychological moment the queen enters and proceeds to manipulate Henry to her advantage. She dramatically offers Henry the cross she has reclaimed from Rosamund. When he "dashes it down," she taunts him all the more: "Saint Cupid, that is too irreverent." Then, having sufficiently aroused him, she tells him that Becket has sent Rosamund "into Godstow nunnery." When Henry leaves in anger and the knights enter, she invites them to strike Becket—"The King would have him." And when the king returns he himself proclaims the famous line, "Will no man free me from this pestilent priest?" Here at least Tennyson probes Henry's susceptibility, but the king's psychological weakness is primarily the means for motivating the story; the relevant action is not in his mind but in his physical response.

The final two scenes take place at Canterbury. Rosamund enters disguised as a monk and approaches Becket. The opening exchange between them indicates Tennyson's desire to expose Becket's character:

Rosamund:	Can I speak with you
	Alone, my father?
Becket:	Come you to confess?

> *Rosamund*: Not now.
> *Becket*:   Then speak; this is my other self,
> Who, like my conscience, never lets me be.

Rosamund argues against Becket's supposed decision to excommunicate Henry, using Becket's own argument against cruelty as a legitimate defense: "I call you cruel." But Becket's "other self" never emerges: "Daughter . . . I shall not do it." In effect, Rosamund reaffirms Becket's innocence rather than reveals his duplicity. Immediately thereafter Salisbury raises the essential question of martyrdom: "He loses half the need of martyrdom / Who will be martyr when he might escape." But even as Becket searches out the reason for his choice, plot again lays claim to action.

Fitzurse and then the knights all threaten Becket. His decision already made, all conflict is now outside character. The knights exit and reenter in order to increase suspense, not provide Becket with an occasion to examine his own motives. While the knights pound on the doors and the monks flee, Becket puts on the vestments of his office. The only issue is when will the martyrdom come. When Salisbury and Grim, another loyal friend, try to coerce Becket to save himself ("We must not force the crown of martyrdom"), Becket ignores them and acts out his part in history. In sum, Tennyson forgoes the psychological implications at the end of the play and completes the action in the form of a traditional denouement. When he is finally struck, Becket delivers a ritualistic benediction:

> I do commend my cause to God, the Virgin,
> Saint Denis of France and Saint Alphege of England,
> And all the tutelar Saints of Canterbury.

As Rosamund runs to him, he finally speaks his last words, "falling on his knees,"

> At the right hand of Power—
> Power and great glory—for thy Church,
>   O Lord—
> Into thy hands, O Lord—into thy hands!

De Brito kills him at last and a "Storm bursts." Cosmic justice responds openly to the offense, as it does in *Lear* and *Macbeth*.

Unlike the modern hero for whom no external values exist, Becket need find no motivation to act within himself. And unlike the hero of *Maud* he acts not in spite of but because of the external world of God and man. Regardless of Tennyson's intent in delineating the progress of Becket's choice, he could not overcome the historical role his character had to play. Nothing short of violating history could have freed him to do with his hero what he had done with the narrator in *Maud* or the legendary figures of the *Idylls*. Louise Rehak has recently compared Tennyson's *Becket* and Eliot's *Murder in the Cathedral*. She notes that at the end of Tennyson's play, "none of the characters learns anything. The conflict is not resolved but merely ends with Becket's death."[19] The conflict between spiritual and temporal powers represented by Henry and Becket may never be completed, but the inner conflict in Becket is never adequately begun. Tennyson describes explicitly Becket's place in the history of England, only implicitly his profound subjective struggle. He may have wanted it both ways, action in plot and action in character, but unlike Shelley he could not pull off the juggler's trick.

Miss Rehak contends that while Eliot's power is "generality" and "religious eloquence," Tennyson's is "psychological realism and political objectivity." Nonetheless, the action is not psychologically motivated so much as it is dictated by Tennyson's acceptance of "the historical record of Becket's conflict with the king." In sum, the play is a sprawling, loosely ordered construct dependent on the demand of historical fact rather than the demands of character. The involved political intrigue, the domestic triangle, the asides on the church, the multiplicity of characters, the frenzied stage action, the surface ironies in plot (e.g., the game of chess) and dialogue (e.g., the references to Rosamund as a bird)—all of these interfere with the development of Becket as a character in the modern sense. On the other hand, Miss Rehak is perfectly right in concluding that "Becket is not a successful drama in the Shakespearean form, where conflict of character should produce some synthesis in terms of plot, but it has something of our current flavour of the drama of alienation in the ironic texture of relationships."[20]

Tennyson wanted to succeed on the stage. When *The Promise of May* met with failure, he bitterly defended it as an effort "to bring the true drama of character and life back again." He thought the drama of England "at its lowest ebb" and cited part of a Milton sonnet: "I did but prompt the age to quit their clogs,/ When straight a barbarous noise environs me/ Of owls and asses, cuckoos, apes and dogs,/ But this is got by casting pearls to hogs."[21] Nevertheless, he retained interest in drama until his death and delighted in Irving's occasional visits to his home. He died with a volume of Shakespeare open in his hands—and fittingly so, because when he wrote for the stage he imitated the dead form of Elizabethan drama and aligned himself with the traditional Irving, who used modern stage techniques most successfully to express an Elizabethan delight in stage illusion.

On the other hand *Maud* is proof enough that Tennyson was sensitive to the discordant movement of the human mind in conflict with itself. He did not consider *Maud* a drama, but the fact that he used the subjective form of the lyric for dramatic purposes implies that he tried to discover a suitable structure for a view of reality not operative in orthodox poetic models. The hybrid structure, dramatic in action and poetic in form, permits a high degree of objectivity but, at the same time, a dramatically charged form. *Maud*'s dramatic intent appears in its fleeting evocations, in the subtle interrelationships of characters in the hero's mind, and in the disjointed but artistically controlled movement of the subjective action. Its poetic inventiveness attests that Tennyson was attempting to dramatize poetically a "soul in action" in the style of a long soliloquy. It is as though the narrator is the author, the actor, and the director of a private mental drama; he alone creates the set and he alone allows the other characters to exist. *Maud* reads more like a poetic version of *Notes From the Underground* than a narrative poem. It is more a poem containing elements of drama than a drama containing elements of poetry. Like Byron and Browning before him, Tennyson simply could not bridge the gap between writing a drama situated in plot and a drama rooted in character.

4

BROWNING'S *A BLOT IN THE 'SCUTCHEON*
AND *PIPPA PASSES*

That arm is wrongly put—and there again—
A fault to pardon in the drawing's lines,
Its body, so to speak: its soul is right.
                    "Andrea Del Sarto"

Tennyson's dramas came at the twilight of his career, Browning's at the dawn of his greatest poetic triumphs. The meager popular response to his plays purged him of his ambition to become a dramatist and so led to his maturation as poet. Indeed, success on the stage may well have aborted Browning's masterful development of the dramatic monologue and assigned him to a lesser place in literary history. And yet, no nineteenth-century poet came closer to writing a modern drama. Unlike Shelley, who unconsciously depicted subjective action in character within the confines of a traditional structure; unlike Byron, who separated himself from the stage to create a "mental theatre"; unlike Tennyson, who ignored the genre when he most fully delineated internal drama, Browning resolutely sought a modern dramatic form communicable on a stage.

In his earnest attempt to gain his laurels as dramatist, Browning's personal loyalties were unavoidably divided. On one hand he was bound to William Charles Macready as his guide and the potential producer of his plays; on the other hand he was devoted to founding his "own notion" of drama. The two loyalties were on a collision course from the beginning of his career and finally resulted in the famous quarrel between the two men over *A Blot in the 'Scutcheon*. Browning was never comfortable writing for Macready and the stage even though he wanted to be a successful playwright. He tried to please both himself and the popular taste and succeeded in neither. His eight plays are a record of his frustrated attempt to avert an inevitable conclusion: there was no place for Browning's theory of drama in the nineteenth-century English theater. His stage plays, written in the popular vein, are obscured by subjective action in character; his closet dramas, written essentially as studies in character, never achieve proper stage form.

The young poet was groping toward a modern concept of drama in which dramatic action is centered in the individual character as an autonomous being who creates his own sense of order and meaning. That is to say, Browning rejected the classical theory of character as agent of plot and attempted to find a dramatic form which could retain the objectivity of drama and yet be a kind of equivalent to the subjective action in a lyric. He sought to break down the barriers between lyric and dramatic form and discover a means of giving subjective matter objective expression. As a result, a tension emerges in Browning's dramas between his romantic sensibility, which emphasizes internal action, and a classical concept of dramatic order, which is a correlative to an established world view. Browning, however, faced a world without affirmed external values and thought of dramatic action in character as the character's struggle to find value and meaning in himself. He faced the problem of creating a drama which could be both individualized and universal, subjective and objective, lyric and dramatic. In other words, he faced the question all modern drama raises: how can there be drama without a social synthesis, a determining ethos and order?

Browning was aware of the inadaptability of his subject to

classical models. He introduced *Paracelsus* in 1835 as a poem rather than a drama, acknowledging that drama could be called drama only if it appears on the stage. The preface to *Strafford* contains the famous statement of his concept of "Action in Character, rather than Character in Action." In its advertisement, he called *Pippa Passes* a poem in a "cheap mode," implying that he was well aware that the piece was somehow illegitimate, part drama and part poem. He similarly realized that *Luria* and *A Soul's Tragedy* were for the study rather than the stage. Yet in all of these he employed dialogue and adhered to many requirements of the drama. For Browning, to cite his often-quoted preface to *Sordello*, the "stress lay on the incidents in the development of a soul: little else is worth study." He was no greater rebel against literary convention than in his experimental dramas, and in *Luria* and *Pippa Passes* he virtually denied all past concepts of dramatic order.

Browning's essays also show that he was aware of the problem of dramatic form. In the year between the publication of *Pippa Passes* and *A Blot in the 'Scutcheon*, he wrote his "Essay on Chatterton" for *The Foreign Quarterly Review*. Donald Smalley, in his edition of the essay, notes how carefully Browning conceived the drama of Chatterton's life and points to many parallels with the more noted "Essay on Shelley," written a decade later.[1] Surely the essay on Shelley shows that Browning had long wrestled with the conflict between subjective matter and objective, dramatic form. He speaks of Shelley as the highest example of "the subjective poet of modern classification." He contrasts Shelley with Shakespeare, the great dramatic poet, arguing that there needs to be a balance of the two. We do not need to know the poet behind *Othello*, he contends, because "his poetry will of necessity be substantive, projected from himself and distinct." In contrast, the modern writer exposes "his own soul." Browning sought the fusion in a new drama whose raw material is the subjective matter of modern literature and whose form is objective in spite of it. He wanted neither the external world of classical drama nor the exclusively lyric world he found in Shelley's poetry. Rather he felt that the dramatist must begin "with this world, as starting point and basis alike," and examine the progress of "a soul in action." He conceived of a drama which would adhere to the public demands of drama and yet focus on individual rather than communal or ritualistic action:

> Nor is there any reason why these two modes of poetic faculty may not issue hereafter from the same poet in successive perfect works, examples of which, according to what are now considered the exigencies of art, we have hitherto possessed in distinct individuals only.

Elizabeth Barrett reinforced Browning's belief in a new art. She wrote him in 1845, "I am inclined to think that we want new forms, as well as thoughts. The old gods are dethroned. Why should we go back to the antique moulds, classical moulds, as they are so improperly called?"[2] He answered with silence.

Browning's own plays may be divided into two groupings, which Park Honan labels "Characters for the Stage" and "Characters for the Study."[3] A good example of the first grouping is *A Blot in the 'Scutcheon.* Structured like the popular "well-made" plays of the period, it contains an internal action in character obscured by the plot. In subject matter *A Blot* is a radical departure from the accepted dramas of the mid-nineteenth century, but in form it follows the narrow conventions of the contemporary stage. Browning's best play for "the study" is *Pippa Passes*, a play modern in both subject and form. Freed from the restrictions of writing expressly for the stage, Browning consciously altered dramatic structure. And in form as well as content, *Pippa Passes* shows that Browning knew and appreciated the differences between a modern idea of drama and the current theater. As with *Cain* and *Werner, Pippa Passes* and *A Blot in the 'Scutcheon* exemplify those differences.

After Browning's first two attempts to write for the stage failed, he sent Macready *The Return of the Druses* in 1840. He received nothing but discouragement as a reply, and he complained, "So once again, dear Macready, I have failed to please you!"[4] The estrangement of actor and author was imminent, as Macready's reaction attests: "I yield to the belief that [Browning] will *never write again*—to any purpose. I fear his intellect is not quite clear."[5] But Browning still wanted to make a place for himself. *A Blot in the 'Scutcheon* marks his last desperate effort to achieve prominence in the theater. Even when he wrote it Browning knew he was compromising his own theory. The note to Macready which preceded the manuscript is in part a signed confession.

> My dear Macready,
> "The luck of the third adventure" is proverbial. I have written a spick and span new Tragedy (a sort of compromise between my own notion and yours—as I understand it, at least) and will send it to you if you are to be bothered so far. There is action in it, drabbing, stabbing, et autres gentillesses,—who knows but the Gods may make me good even yet?[6]

And the play itself is the clearest example among Browning's dramas of the incompatibility of his notion of drama and theater taste.

Like *The Cenci, A Blot in the 'Scutcheon* contains two actions, one centered in character and one in plot. Browning consciously emphasized physical action ("drabbing, stabbing, et autres gentillesses") in order to please Macready, who had condemned *Strafford* for its "meanness of plot and occasional obscurity."[7] As a result, the essential internal action centered in Tresham is hopelessly absorbed by melodramatic plotting. And yet in content, *A Blot* is revolutionary. The love affair of Mertoun and Mildred does not conform to traditional concepts of morality. The real action rests in Tresham's gradual awareness that his moral judgments are too limited and, above all, in his painful recognition that the blot in the 'scutcheon is his own unnatural love for his sister. The moral "fall" is not Mildred's but her brother's. The internal action is unlike any of the dramas popular on the contemporary stage and unlike classical drama in that it does not affirm but defies established social and moral rules. But whereas the internal action in the play is expressly modern, the structure is not. The external plot is an imitation of popular stage pieces and works in direct opposition to the action in character. Externally the play is a second-rate melodrama, a last example of sentimental romantic tragedy; and the radical moral statement implicit in the underlying action is not apparent.

A *Blot in the 'Scutcheon* parallels earlier imitations of Shakespearean drama but is structured like a "well-made" play. The plot echoes *Romeo and Juliet*, but it is primarily a melodrama in the popular vein. The mixture of the popular notion of tragedy (in essence melodrama with a great deal of stage action) and the "well-made" play denies Browning the opportunity to explore action in character, and the implicit conflict between form and matter in the play sentenced it to certain failure. Although the *pièce bien faite* did not reach its fullest influence in Europe and England until Sardou began a spectacular career with *Les Premières Armes de Figaro* in 1859, the "well-made" play had been influential since Scribe began writing in 1811. "In England," Stephen S. Stanton has observed, "Scribe's eminently translatable and actable comedies began to appear in 1819."[8] More important, Bulwer-Lytton had made use of the structural technique of the "well-made" play in several of his plays, particularly *Richelieu* and *Money*. Bulwer-Lytton was a very great success at the box office and had a sizable influence on the drama. Macready, of course, knew him intimately and in part depended upon the popular Lord Lytton for much of his repertoire. It is no wonder, then, that when Browning decided to "compromise" his notion of tragedy in order to please Macready, he turned to the structure of the "well-made" play.

Stanton lists the following elements in the plot of a "well-made" play: 1) a secret known to the audience but unknown to several characters which forms the basis of the plot; 2) the use of mounting suspense (usually caused by "contrived entrances and exits, letters and other devices"); 3) a number of "ups and downs in the hero's fortunes, caused by his conflict with an adversary"; 4) the disclosure of secrets to the antagonist resulting in "the lowest and highest point in the hero's adventures"; 5) a misunderstanding recognized by the audience but not by the characters; 6) a "credible denouement"; 7) "the reproduction of the overall action pattern in the individual acts."[9] *A Blot* not only follows the overall pattern, it also adheres to the specific steps in the dramatic method.

The first act is basically exposition. The secret is disclosed to the audience: Mildred and Mertoun have engaged in a secret love affair unknown to Mildred's brother, Earl Tresham. We also learn that Tresham is haughty and devoted to the family name, that Mildred is suffering pangs of conscience because of the illicit love, and that Mertoun is unwilling to acknowledge guilt—"I think upon your purity / And utter ignorance of guilt." Guendolen and Austin are also introduced. Guendolen serves to further the plot at times, and both she and Austin provide ironic comments through their ignorance of the real situation. When Tresham praises the unblemished character of Mertoun, for example, Guendolen says that Tresham is bewitched by Mertoun's "purity" and that "Witchcraft's a fault in him." At the end of the first act the action itself begins; this too follows the formula. Mertoun and Mildred agree to meet "one night more." There is a battle of wits, in a sense, as Mertoun, playing the part of a suitor, plans to meet Mildred under cover of darkness one more time, and Tresham unwittingly plans a union already consummated.

Concealed within the external plot, the hidden conflict in Tresham is also established. On the surface, he is eager to make the match but insists upon one qualification—"Mildred's hand is hers to give / Or to refuse." There is a suggestion of his more than natural admiration for Mildred in his description of her:

> How pure yet passionate, how calm yet kind,
> How grave yet joyous, how reserved yet free,
> As light where friends are—how imbued with lore
> The world most prizes, yet the simplest, yet
> The . . . one might know I talked of Mildred—thus
> We brothers talk! (I.ii.178-83)

Ironically, as he pleads Mildred's case to Mertoun, Tresham exposes his own subconscious love for her. She is not quite fourteen and "has never known / A mother's care." In being "father" to her he has developed a passion for her apparent at first only in his praise of her as a perfect match for Mertoun. The situation activates his latent attraction to her. Yet Browning necessarily focused on the external plot so that the play would hold interest for an audience. As a result the play seems conventional and sentimental.

The two levels of plot and action separate more decidedly in Act 2. Often in a "well-made" play, according to Stanton, "the hero is loved by two women." In *A Blot* Mildred is loved by her brother and Mertoun, and on the surface the conflict revolves around the superficially ironic situation: Tresham wants Mildred to marry Mertoun but is unaware that they are already lovers and that marriage would be only a sham. The real conflict in Tresham is almost undecipherable in the entanglements of the plot. The hero appears to be Mertoun, who tries in Act 2 to unravel his impossible predicament. At the beginning of the act a contrived obstacle interferes with his plans—again, true to the "well-made" formula. The loyal retainer, Gerard, tells Lord Tresham of a mysterious person who has visited Mildred's chamber at midnight every night for a month. But Tresham's comfortable confidence in Mildred's nobility does not permit him to believe the worst: "Gerard, some wretched fool / Dares pry into my sister's privacy!" But, alas, the evidence is too strong. The mounting suspense characteristic of the "well-made" play is actualized by stock gimmicks: the contrived entrance of Gerard; the reference to the signal used by Mertoun and Mildred—"a lamp that's full i' the midst, / Under a red square in the painted glass / Of Lady Mildred's. . . ."; Tresham's counter schemes.

The irony intensifies when Guendolen enters and tells Tresham how she spent the night trying to convince Mildred to accept Mertoun. True to character, Tresham reacts in a way suitable to Guendolen's description of him in Act 1:

> He's proud, confess; so proud with brooding o'er
> The light of his interminable line,

> An ancestry with men all paladins,
> And women all. . . .

(I.iii.314-17)

On the surface he seems disturbed by Mildred's effect on the
family name. He humiliates her, and we see the emergence of a
supposed conflict in him between his "brother's love" and his
ancestral pride. When he attempts to erase the "blot" by reveng-
ing himself on the villainous paramour, Mildred will not confess
her lover's name; and the conflict becomes twofold. Now Mildred
is torn between her self-acknowledged "guilt" in the love affair
and her loyalty to Mertoun. The second act ends, however, with
Guendolen's optimistic prediction that the situation can be resolved, the "false hope" in the "well-made" plot.

But submerged beneath the external action of the second act,
another action develops in Tresham. He may appear to play out
a stock role in the plot as an avenging hero, wronged, yet doomed
by his own impulsiveness. Browning, however, hints at a deeper
motivation for his acts. Tresham is totally demoralized by his
sister's "fallen" state. What disturbs him is not so much the
"blot" she puts on the 'scutcheon as the proof that "she's un-
chaste." When he accuses Mildred of the moral infraction he
points to a line of Latin in a book. When he calls her to his side
to translate it for her ("Love conquers all things"), he is repelled
by the touch of her body—"Don't lean on me." He asks her
whose love she should esteem most and answers for her,

> Mildred, I do believe a brother's love
> For a sole sister must exceed them all.
> . . . .
> —I think, am sure, a brother's love exceeds
> All the world's love in its unworldliness.

(II.ii.157-58, 190-91)

His unrecognized desire reveals itself in a confused expression
of jealousy and passion—"So close you live and yet so far apart!"
He accuses Mildred of "Wild illicit ties" and is incapable of for-
giving her. But in exaggerating her "guilt" he reveals his own:
"No lighter of the signal-lamp her quick / Foul breath near

quenches in hot eagerness / To mix with breath as foul!" He accuses her above all of not even being faithful to her lover, in that she "calmly gives her lover up / As means to wed the Earl that she may hide / Their intercourse the surelier." In sum, Tresham is incapable of rational thought; his latent incestuous love explodes into the violence of revenge. But because he plays out a central role in the surface intrigue, Tresham's motivation is never fully examined; he seems but an agent of plot.

In the third act the plot completes the pattern of a "well-made" play. After the see-saw action of Act 2, the *peripeteia* occurs. This, too, depends upon the machination of plot. Tresham happens to be wandering in the orchard at midnight when he asks himself, "Why came I here? What must I do?" A bell strikes, and suddenly he is illuminated. "Ah, I catch /—Woods, rivers, plains, I catch your meaning now, / And I obey you! Hist! This tree will serve." Cloaked and disguised, Mertoun arrives to wait for Mildred's signal. As one might guess, Tresham challenges him to combat and Mertoun is fatally stabbed. According to the "well-made" play structure, after the *peripeteia* the protagonist suffers a crushing defeat, which should be triggered by a revelation of the secret. When Tresham is accused by Mertoun of being the author of the tragedy, he "suffers a crushing defeat" through his own ironic victory:

> Mertoun, haste
> And anger have undone us. 'Tis not you
> Should tell me for a novelty you're young,
> Thoughtless, unable to recall the past.
> Be but your pardon ample as my own! (III.i.125-29)

In this recognition scene, the *anagnorisis*, Tresham suffers "unexpected loss," and "the denouement follows at once, with appropriate dispensation to the good and the bad characters." Mildred dies to "be sure of [Mertoun] forever!" Tresham dies from poison he has taken and says while dying, "Vengeance is God's, not man's. Remember me!" The play falls into hopeless sentimentality and melodrama.

Almost unrecognized amid the resolving action of the plot, the subjective climax is reached in Tresham. Mertoun makes him promise to tell Mildred that he dies loving her. In the second scene Tresham comes to Mildred's chamber to tell her of the death. In this final confrontation Tresham finally suspects the hidden motivation of his acts. At first he recalls his childhood with Mildred—"How we waded—years ago— / After those water-lilies. . . ." When Mildred guesses what has happened, she at first pardons her brother, but he cannot accept it, "You cannot, Mildred!" He admits that he struck Mertoun without permitting him to explain: "Had I but glanced, where all seemed turbidest / Had gleaned some inlet to the calm beneath . . . and you—say on— / You curse me?" In her reply she hints at the dark cause:

> There! Do not think too much upon the past!
> The cloud that's broke was all the same a cloud
> While it stood up between my friend and you;
> You hurt him 'neath its shadow. . . .   (III.ii.337-40)

As she speaks her last words she falls on his neck. She blesses Tresham but will not forgive him, suggesting that she understands that he was driven into the murder. Ironically, his suppressed passion is realized by her locked arms around his neck:

> *Guendolen.*   She's dead!
>   Let me unlock her arms!
> *Tresham.*   She threw them thus
>   About my neck, and blessed me, and then died:
>   You'll let them stay now, Guendolen!   (III.ii.347-50)

When he dies, frothing at the mouth, he hints at the horror of his own recognition:

> There are blind ways provided, the foredone
> Heart-weary player in this pageant-world
> Drops out by, letting the main masque defile
> By the conspicuous portal. . . .   (III.ii.363-66)

The action in character is so clouded by the external plot that it is almost indistinguishable. There are several incisive requirements of the "well-made" play that automatically negate any serious treatment of internal action, and yet Browning's interest was with such action. Stanton provides us with a clear explanation of the artistic problem: "It is to be noted that the will of the characters in this type of drama [the "well-made" play] is always subordinate to the exigencies of the plot and to the artifices employed by the author."[10] Browning tries throughout to stretch the bounds of the pattern in order to examine the subjective action, but the stage action resides purely in plot and depends upon the entangled situation of the proposed marriage, the knowledge of the loyal Gerard, the use of disguises, the clandestine last meeting of the lovers and the unraveling of the surface complications caused by the secret affair. In short, the moral questions raised are too revolutionary, too complex, too individual to be dealt with in the confines of the structure. Superficially, the play seems a feeble imitation of *Romeo and Juliet* placed in the "well-made" pattern. Actually, Browning's play is very unShakespearean. The star-crossed lovers in Shakespeare's play suffer at the hands of fate; the stars foretell the impending doom caused by the fatal family feuds. There is no question of immorality in the play; rather innocent love is destroyed by social disorder, by the unnatural feuding. Because the pseudo-Elizabethan matter of Browning's play is so apparent, the play's viewpoint seems orthodox. But fate is not the author of the tragedy, nor is the focus really on the lovers' hopeless situation. There is a genuine conflict between traditional morality and the moral position taken in the play. Mertoun and Mildred, in spite of their indiscretion, are clearly innocent of a moral infraction. And Tresham, whose outrage seems to stem from his indignant moral sense, is proven "guilty." The tragedy is caused neither by fate nor the lovers' actions, but by Tresham's latent incestuous love for his sister. His jealousy is the blot in the 'scutcheon, not Mildred's affair.

There are examples in the play of Browning's attempt to develop the moral issue. At the end of Act 1, Mertoun and Mildred engage in a debate about the moral implications of their affair. Mertoun counters Mildred's feeling of "guilty" love with significant arguments:

> must I now renounce
> My reason, blind myself to light, say truth
> Is false and lie to God and my own soul?
> Contempt were all of this! (I.iii.477-80)

Then, too, Guendolen is used to foil Tresham's harsh judgments. She stands by Mildred in spite of Tresham's and Austin's condemnations. The use of parallel characters like Austin and Guendolen is characteristic of the "well-made" play, but Browning uses Guendolen in more than a perfunctory way. She not only motivates the physical action and provides superficial irony by her naive comments in Act 1, she also accepts the burden of the moral choice when she encounters Mildred at the end of Act 2 and judges her "free from all that heap / Of sins." Being free from a blind loyalty to the family name and conventional morality, she is capable of making the right moral judgment.

Browning also tried to escape from mere dependence on plot in other ways. He used setting (as interpreted by individual characters) as a means of internal revelation. When Mertoun leaves Mildred at the end of Act 1, Mildred sees nature participate in his departure: "His foot is on the yew-bough; the turf / Receives him: now the moonlight as he runs / Embraces him—but he must go—is gone." At the beginning of Act 3 Tresham also personifies nature, and the contrast between his vision and Mildred's is a striking revelation. Mertoun melts into nature and is received by it. When Tresham tries to escape into "the heath," "the orchard, dells and bosky paths," the "green wildwood depths," he discovers that they drive him back into conflict with himself: "The very river put / Its arms about me and conducted me / To this detested spot." He speaks of his family line from which "would proceed / No poison-tree, to thrust, from hell its roots, / Hither and thither its strange snaky arms." His warped mental state is envisioned by projections into the world of nature. The excessive description, with its sensual quality, implies that family honor is but a surface reason for his actions. But the scene is rapidly covered over by the stock character of the events which immediately follow: the mysteriously cloaked villain, the challenge delivered in bombastic language, the removal of Mertoun's mask, the death of the lover.

Tresham's repentance comes too easily. One minute he stabs Mertoun; a few lines later he suffers remorse. Too much of the dialogue belongs to Mertoun, too little to Tresham's response to the accusations. Mertoun raises the moral issue:

> What right was yours to set
> The thoughtless foot upon her life and mine,
> And then say, as we perish, "Had I thought,
> All had gone otherwise"? We've sinned and die:
> Never you sin, Lord Tresham! for you'll die,
> And God will judge you. (III.i.152-57)

But the issue does not materialize in Tresham. Rather the appearance of Gerard, Austin, and Guendolen interrupts the scene. And later when Tresham encounters Mildred and the truth begins to break upon his consciousness, the sensational melodrama of the ending overpowers the self-discovery.

Browning failed in *A Blot* because he raised questions that cannot be examined within the structure he used. James McCormick has described the failure accurately:

> The poet was unable to carry conviction on an interesting moral issue with plays that were written in a sentimental Shakespearian structure and tradition. In spite of the fact that he used many of the conventional heart throbs, he failed as a popular playwright.[11]

Browning's interest was in character, where the moral question must ultimately reside; but to trace the "incidents in the development of a soul" there was in his age only an empty stage as medium. Once he discovered that truth his enthusiasm for theatrical glory gradually faded.

Browning had put his faith in the production of *A Blot*, but after it flopped miserably and *Colombe's Birthday* proved even more disastrous, he wrote Elizabeth Barrett, "I like 'Pippa' better than anything else I have done yet. . . ."[12] Perhaps he recognized how severely he had prostituted himself in writing *A Blot*, how shamelessly he had flirted with a stage audience Elizabeth once described as "the Great unwashed who can't read."[13] The experimental plays that completed his dramatic canon—*A Soul's Tragedy*, *Luria*, and *In a Balcony*—indicate that Browning had had his fill of the theater if not of drama. For a brief period he tried once again to do something new with the genre, but none of the late plays is as innovative and venturesome as his first serious experimental drama, *Pippa Passes*.

None of the heroes in the major plays we have studied is a traditional protagonist: Beatrice is alienated from even her God; Cain defies the cosmic justice which condemns him; the speaker in *Maud* moves chaotically through a series of moods to an uncertain end. Cain's and Maud's lovers are antiheroes—one through conviction, one through ineffectuality. In *Pippa Passes* the traditional concept of character disappears altogether, and we are left with what Roma A. King, Jr., calls "a composite character—man, Everyman—conceived as so complex and at odds with himself that he can be portrayed—on the stage, at least—only as a cast of characters."[14] The fragmentation of values is so complete, the disintegration of the social importance of character so total, that one character is no longer sufficient to express the dramatic vision. The cause-and-effect ritual of classical tragedy, resting assuredly on a firm belief in an ordered world, has broken into a series of dramatic actions.

In most of his dramas, Browning is caught between dependence on old, accepted forms and the absolute necessity of breaking from traditional patterns in order to be true to his artistic purpose. Liberated from the mandates of the "well-made" plot, he is able to explore in *Pippa* what E. D. H. Johnson refers to as "tensions antecedent to action."[15] Rather than employing multiple characters in numerous stage actions as he had done in his first drama, *Strafford*, Browning concentrates on a few characters shown in an "infinite moment." Four episodes, completely self-contained and yet contributing to the whole, replace the arrangements of incidents in a typical plot. In effect, we have four one-act plays, four separate actions, developed autonomously yet couched precariously within one sustained action. ("I have entered into sympathy / With these four," Cleon says, "running these into one soul.") Browning's unique conception allows little opportunity for ordinary exposition or plot development within the internal episodes. In each the conflict is already initiated, the crisis begun. The rising action and elaborate plotting so necessary to the "well-made" play would be impossible in Browning's structural pattern.

But Browning's scheme had its risks, and he confronted a serious problem: how was he to achieve unity in a structure where episodes replace orthodox cause-and-effect plotting and the protagonist dissolves into a multiplicity of characters? Pippa was to be the solution. She catalyzes the action in all the episodes and is the structural center of the play, and yet she is certainly not a character in the ordinary sense. She links the episodes but is only peripherally involved in them; she is the only continuous character but not the protagonist. Nothing happens to her, even though she is the only mobile character, nor does she confront any other character directly. Except for her opening speech, she is all but transparent in the play. Browning imagined her less a character than a structural device designed to relate the divergent actions and trigger some kind of responses in major characters. She is, as King has said, "more a force, an impetus to action, than a character."[16]

Her opening soliloquy makes us aware of the concrete presence of the town, and provides a realistic frame for the dramatic action. It also locates the sites of the ensuing episodes (the shrub-house, "*our* turret," Jules's house overlooking "Orcana valley") and identifies the sordid activities in the town. Unlike the first act of a typical play, the beginning of *Pippa Passes* does not create suspense or provide motivation for plot, except in the loosest sense. Rather, by means of Pippa's naive introduction to the main characters, "Asolo's Four Happiest Ones," Browning prefigures the internal conflicts in character, not the machinations of plot. As Pippa envisions her day in terms of weather—potential rain on Ottima's shrub-house, an overcast moon over Jules and Phene, mist surrounding Luigi and his mother, a storm on Monsignor's villa—she draws into focus the four separate actions to follow.

Because Pippa is a transparent figure lacking the complexity of a fully developed *dramatis persona*, she can serve as a kind of correlative for the subjective struggles she unwittingly "resolves." Even granting that she is a far more substantial character than critics have traditionally allowed, she is elemental, possessing neither the ability nor the experience to pass moral judgments accurately. Her essential simplicity contrasts with the complex mental states of the characters she changes. King is correct in proposing that her only real function is her "passing" from encounter to encounter. Rather than being "God's messenger," a visitant from another world, she becomes the articulation of the "other voice" in each of the characters, a pole in the internal dialectic we have noted in other works. Her own high hope explains the drama that unfolds: "Untwine me from the mass / Of deeds which make up life, one deed / Power shall fall short in or exceed!" In the dramatic pattern, Pippa fulfills her wish in other characters, presenting them with the possibility of choice: she permits them to act and to escape from the garbled "mass / Of deeds which make up life." Like Cain's Lucifer, but far less directly, she rescues others from self-destructive stasis.

The overall movement of the play centers on Pippa and the way she spends her day, but the individual episodes carry the real action. In these, if not in the drama as a whole, Browning achieves dramatic power; and none of the episodes reaches the concentration and force of the first. Sebald's opening song is an arresting paradox, exposing his subjective turmoil. Pippa's omnipotent day is juxtaposed with his inability to distinguish night from day: "Day's a-blaze with eyes, think! / Deep into the night, drink!" And Sebald and Ottima are in fact caught between "drink" and "think." Intoxicated with passion, they have murdered Luca, and the day now brings that fact into full focus. For Browning the drama resides in the consequence of murder, not the deed itself. We begin then with Sebald's devastating subjective nausea and Ottima's contrasting moral detachment from both murder and illicit love.

In order to concentrate on individual characters in all the episodes, Browning restricts setting, employing it as the symbolic projection of internal action. Ottima and Sebald are inside the shrub-house, where the body of Luca lies visible on the floor. The emerging of conscience in Sebald is contradicted by Ottima's frigid unconcern. He fears the day; she greets it: "let us see!" Sebald's view of the world is colored by his own sense of guilt. He recalls the normal activities around Luca's house—"country girls / Were noisy, washing garments in the brook, / Hinds drove the slow white oxen up the hills"—but his remembrance of the natural setting is destroyed by the animated horror of Luca's house: "mute," "would ope no eye," "Rough," "rusty," "Silent as death," "blind in a flood of light." His memory is affected by his own sense of spiritual death. The house "blind in a flood of light" parallels the paradox of his own song, as the light of day brings to him a spiritual darkness. Ottima suffers no subjective crisis. Her language is free of metaphorical complexity and emotional disturbance. Consequently, she sees,

> Ah, the clear morning! I can see St. Mark's;
> That black streak is the belfry. Stop: Vicenza
> Should lie . . . there's Padua, plain enough,
>   that blue! (I.28-30)

She responds to the physical beauty of the day and talks almost like a tour guide, while Sebald probes the darkness of Luca's house, where "You were plotting one thing there, / Nature, another outside."

Sebald is all but unaware of the physical day. He sees only "a night with a sun added." While Ottima speaks of generalized objects—towns, the church and belfry—Sebald's observations are particularized and painfully personal. He notices "that bruised plant, I bruised / In getting through the lattice yestereve" and "my elbow's mark / I' the dust o' the sill." In dramatic form, the day reveals both the tension in Sebald and the conflict between the two lovers. The action consists of Ottima's efforts to free Sebald from his own conscience.

Sebald projects his sense of spiritual despair into the view he sees from the window, so Ottima orders him to "shut out the world." When she is alone with him and he cannot envision his guilt in the outer world, she can compete with his remorse. In the isolation of the closed room, he can turn only to her, separated from the human community outside. He wants a confirmation of the guilt from Ottima: "How do you bear yourself? Let's out / With all of it." But for all his intense prompting, Ottima has only an unemotional response: "Best never speak of it." When Sebald's remorse evolves into a climactic fragment—"Say, once and always, Luca was a wittol, I am his cut-throat, you are . . ."— Ottima is equal to the situation: "Here's the wine." From the beginning, neither character can respond to the other. At first Sebald sits stunned, incapable of action and all but unaware of what Ottima says. Then, when he tries to communicate his remorse and involve her, she constantly ignores his efforts. At one point, she calmly describes "Benet the Capuchin" walking. When Sebald raises the moral question, Ottima disregards it as dispassionately as she does Benet, "the brown cold piece" against the "plastered wall" of the church.

The dramatic conflict in and between the two characters is intensified after the lattice is shut. A kind of mock ritual develops. There is the drinking of the wine, Sebald insisting on the white rather than the red. Then Ottima recounts the affair, almost delighting in remembering. To Sebald, Ottima's account is a confession. He at first warns Ottima not to create suspicion ("that is, not make more / Parade of warmth, childish officious coil, / Than yesterday"); but when he ends with the realization that "we still could lose each other, were we not tied by this," he triggers a reaction in Ottima. She insists that they are not "tied" by the

murder but by "Love!" She obscures his sense of guilt by recalling the May night "Under the green ascent of sycamore." If the
corpse had been present then, she pleads, what difference would
it have made? She epitomizes her belief in the murder by saying
she would "Dare . . . go back and hold / His two dead hands, and
say, 'I hate you worse, / Luca, than. . . .' " As Sebald probes the
profound moral implications of the murder, Ottima continues to
concern herself with pragmatic needs: where should the body
be carried? Sebald recants the whole business—"That this were
undone! Killing! Kill the world / So Luca lives again!—ay, lives
to sputter / His fulsome dotage on you"; but Ottima is magnificently unconcerned:

> This dusty pane might serve for looking-glass.
> Three, four—four grey hairs! Is it so you said
> A plait of hair should wave across my neck?
> No—this way.   (I.121-24)

Sebald looks to the future to redeem somehow "the wild reck-
less wicked days flown over," but even while he confesses, Ottima
seduces him. He confuses past and present: "Why must you *lean*
across till your cheeks *touched*?" When he unconsciously expresses his sin, she demands that he acknowledge her presence—
"look at me while I speak to you." Boldly glorying in her "sin,"
she captures the consequence of their love, "pleasure and crime
together." She recreates the scene of their passion in the "garden
silence" in order to seduce him and counters his recantation with
the question, "Who stammered—'Yes, I love you'?" Gradually,
Sebald falls prey to Ottima's charms and tries to still the voice
of his conscience. He rejects the present and relives the "crown-
ing night." When he begins to weaken, Ottima adds heat to the
fire, recalling the violent rain storm: "swift ran the searching
tempest," "Some bright white shaft / Burned thro' the pine-
roof," "Plunged and replunged," "Broke the thunder like a whole
sea overhead." She turns his moral doubts into a testament of
love, arouses his passion ("Breathe slow, speak slow! / Do not

lean on me!"), and insists that he already answered the moral question when,

> Who said, "Let death come now! 'Tis right to die!
> Right to be punished! Naught completes such bliss
> But woe!" Who said that? (I.207-09)

Ottima transforms his guilt into passion and clouds his conscience. She tightens her hold, recalling that he took her locks " 'twixt both your humid lips. / My hair is fallen now: knot it again!" Suddenly Ottima brings him back to the present—she has won out over his conscience:

> Ottima: Bind it thrice about my brow;
> Crown me your queen, your spirit's arbitress,
> Magnificent in sin. Say that!
> Sebald: I crown you
> My great white queen, my spirit's arbitress,
> Magnificent . . . (I.216-20)

In everything Ottima maintains her composure. Her direct orders (which also begin the scene) are juxtaposed against her passionate description of the "garden silence": "knot it again!" "Bind it thrice about my brow," "Say that!" Then Pippa passes:

> The year's at the spring
> The day's at the morn
> Morning's at seven;
> The hill-side's dew-pearled;
> The lark's on the wing;
> The snail's on the thorn;
> God's in his heaven—
> All's right with the world! (I.221-28)

The garbled complexity of the dialogue between the lovers, the circular and indefinite movement of the scene, are thrown into bold relief by the utter simplicity of Pippa's song. The effect upon Sebald is electric—"Do you hear that? Who spoke? / You, you spoke!" In a sense, the song is the reassertion of Sebald's own conscience: it strips away all the entanglements in Sebald's mind and clarifies the moral issue. Throughout the episode Sebald is aware of his depraved state, but he is rendered incapable of action by his involvement with Ottima. Now, at the moment when Sebald is lost in the remembrance of the garden scene, Pippa unwittingly reactivates his conscience. He can respond because Pippa is a part of himself, the "other voice" freed from external involvements. Sebald suddenly becomes aware of physical horrors: "Go get your clothes on—dress those shoulders," "Wipe off that paint." He projects his awareness into Ottima's physical decadence: "the blank cheek," "the cloven brow and puckered chin," "the very hair . . . a dead web!"

Until this moment Sebald has been unable either to love Ottima or be free from her; he is imprisoned in a limbo where action is impossible. Pippa's song obliterates the rationalizations, complexities, and enticements which quell the conscience. And when he confesses his detestation, Ottima is forced to act too. At first she sees no mystery in Pippa's voice. She identifies Pippa as "The little ragged girl"; and, remembering that Pippa works at the silk mill, she turns from her passionate appeals—the spell obviously broken—and dangles the "ten silk-mills" before Sebald. When it is obvious that Sebald will not rescind, her emotional calm is shattered. She is shaken out of her lethargic self-confidence. And when Sebald's rejection of her overshadows all other concerns, she seemingly finds a depth to her love that has not appeared before. When all external matters are diminished, her love for Sebald is released. Latent from the beginning, her true love now finds expression. She exceeds mere sensuality: "Lean on my breast—*not as a breast.*"

Ironically, Sebald is free to kill himself. Jacob Korg sees this as no more than the recovery of will:

> Sebald's speeches after Pippa's song are those of a man who is free, but not saved. He can now recognize Ottima's trickery, he can distinguish moral values, he knows his own sin, and accepts the principle of justice that compels him to suffer for it. Nevertheless, he goes into the "black, fiery"

waters of bitter remorse. In spite of Ottima's final, significant cry, "Not me—to Him, O God, be merciful!", there is no sign of redemption here.[17]

Perhaps. Redemption, we may say, is simply not the issue. In their separate choices Ottima and Sebald are a divided soul; but both are freed from passivity to act. Nothing else matters. In spite of his admiration, H. B. Charlton expresses dismay over the fact that in all of the episode there is never any mention of social justice. The police are never interested, he complains, even though the most naive of people in the town, Pippa, is aware of the illicit love affair. When Ottima wants Sebald to help remove the body, it is because the corpse is "aesthetically an eyesore, not because there is a corporate institution, moral or legal, called the law."[18] But precisely because the action does reside in character, whether the police come or not is totally irrelevant. Completion of the external action is not a necessity except as it relates to character; whether Ottima commits suicide along with Sebald or not ("There, there, both deaths presently"?) does not matter either.

The transition between the first two episodes signals a new interest—the artist and his art—and draws the focus back to the general movement of the play. The interlude also provides a backdrop for the dramatic action. The realistic detail—Shramm's pipe, the setting, the references to specific people in the town (especially Natalia)—continues the method Browning has used of grounding subjective matter in an objective world. When the students characterize "this strutting stone-squarer," they do so with concrete references to places and objects: Passagno, Canova's gallery, the "Psiche-fanciulla," "the unfinished 'Pietà.' " Similarly, they give detailed descriptions of Phene: "a true islander," "a daughter of Natalia," "sea-eagle." They describe only physical beings and a physical world, not realizing the spiritual possibilities involved. The students speak with unknowing wisdom. When they speak of Jules's art derogatorily, they accurately describe what Jules himself discovers with much more profound insight later. When the Fifth Student see Jules coming, he unknowingly illuminates the internal conflict by observing "Half his hair in storm and half in calm."

The dramatic action in the Jules-Phene episode is similar to that in the other three. Jules's art is servile imitation and dead perfection; and, like Ottima and Sebald, the artist is unable to free his soul. Like Andrea del Sarto, he is a victim of his own skill and creates artifacts rather than art. Phene to him represents the ideal model:

> I over lean
> This length of hair and lustrous front; they turn
> Like an entire flower—upward: eyes, lips, last
> Your chin—no, last your throat turns. . . .   (II.4-7)

The objects in the studio are the visual record of Jules's art, and as he talks continually about his work, Phene sits quietly, a dramatic contrast to the dead statuary which surrounds her.

The action evolves gradually, Jules talking and delighting in his room full of artifacts. He waits for Phene to respond as she examines the room: the books full of dead names ("A Coluthus, writ . . . by Bessarion's scribe," "This Odyssey in coarse black vivid type") and the statues ("better that will look/ When cast in bronze," "Hippolyta, / Naked upon her bright Numidian horse," "A Greek, in Athens"). But Phene is a real life-force in a room ironically resplendent with mock vitality: the Greek's "palpitating arch / Of hands and arms," "The quick drip of wine," "drenched leaves," "Violet and parsley crowns." She understands almost nothing about the art; she is not the Hippolyta Jules's mind creates, not the "one form," "the human archetype." In stressing the complete incongruity between Jules's imagined Phene and the real Phene, Browning probes at Jules's failure as an artist bound to frozen forms; Phene's silence throws the burden of proof on the artist—for her the "Greek" is dead.

Phene responds only to Jules himself ("You creature with the eyes"), not the art. Whereas she sees the human element in Jules, he thinks of her as "Hippolyta," an ironic contrast to the poor model and prostitute she really is. He ignites her spirit, and she extends her warm hand of reality—"Keep me so, / Above the world!"—in exchange for his marble. What he "perfects" in illusion ("the tree, the flower—or take the fruit,— / Some rosy shape, continuing the peach, / Carved beewise o'er its bough") she becomes in the flesh.

Then Phene recites the poem Bluphocks has written for Lutwyche: "Love a man or hate a man / Supremely; thus my love began." The message is grossly literal and direct:

> Once, when I loved, I would enlace
> Breast, eyelids, hands, feet, form and face
> Of her I loved, in one embrace—
> As if by mere love I could love immensely!
> Once, when I hated, I would plunge
> My sword, and wipe with the first lunge
> My foe's whole life out like a sponge—
> As if by mere hate I could hate intensely!
> . . . .
> When I love most, Love is disguised
> In Hate; and when Hate is surprised
> In Love then I hate most. . . .   (II.207-14, 228-30)

Confronted with the truth, Jules's whole illusory world crumbles before him. Like Maud's lover, he wants to escape reality and flee "To Ancona—Greece—some isle!" He gives gold to Phene, money being no temptation. Most importantly, he determines to sell "these, my casts / And books and medals." He admits the failure of his art, a necessary step in the redemptive process; but he cannot "by mere Love . . . love immensely!" Stripped of illusion, rendered hopeless, unable to identify either with Phene or his art, he wishes revenge and then oblivion.

Pippa's song does for him what it did for Sebald. By the unadorned plainness of the story it tells it rejuvenates his spirit. Pippa sings of Kate, "who renounced / The crown of Cyprus to be lady here / At Asolo" to "only a page that carols unseen." The barrier between Phene and Jules is Jules's preconceived notion of the woman he would love like the "Psiche-fanciulla." Now his sophisticated image of the ideal woman is destroyed by Pippa's song:

> Why should we always choose the page's part?
> Here is a woman with utter need of me—
> I find myself queen here, it seems!   (II.285-87)

Loosed from his pride and empowered to act, he breaks "these
paltry models up / To begin Art afresh." Pippa's song shatters
his esoteric dreams and presents him with the potential of life
in the here and now ("as now—as now!"), in the immediate
presence of Phene, whom he holds in his arms.

What will happen to Jules? Monsignor later mentions that
Jules "never had a clearly conceived Ideal within his brain until
today." He recognizes Jules's past failure: "a fatal expertness."
Noting that Jules has turned to painting, he hopes the young
artist will found a school like Correggio. He gives the possible
end of Jules's new found devotion:

> Foolish Jules! and yet, after all, why
> foolish? He may—probably will—fail egregiously;
> but if there should arise a new painter, will it not
> be some such way, by a poet now, or a musician
> (spirits who have conceived and perfected an Ideal
> through some other channel), transferring it to
> this, and escaping our conventional roads by pure
> ignorance of them. . . .   (IV.62-69)

Jules's end is, in fact, not important, only that he has seen "One
mountain for a moment in the dusk." The drama in character is
completed when Jules commits himself "To begin Art afresh."
What finally results from the decision is extraneous to the action.

In the interlude with Bluphocks, Browning tries as he does
throughout to relate the episodes to the general action, the passing of Pippa's day. Within the short conversation between the
English vagabond and the policemen we get some dark references
to the Monsignor, who appears in the fourth section, and necessary information about Luigi as a Carbonari. We also return to
the first episode when the First Policeman says, "I have been no-
ticing a house yonder, this long while: not a shutter unclosed
since morning!" The Second Policeman informs him of the prob-
able reason ("Old Luca Gaddi . . . dozes again, after having bid-

den young Sebald, the foreigner, set his wife to playing draughts"), and it becomes apparent again how compact and limited the world of Asolo is. When Bluphocks signals the appearance of Luigi and his mother, the scene shifts inside the turret on the hill above Asolo.

In each episode, Browning rejects the wide stage as setting and limits the playing area to the small scope of Luca's shrubhouse, Jules's room, and now the turret. The playing area permits no broad stage actions and magnifies the simplest acts, such as the dust falling from the window in the Ottima-Sebald section. The ensuing conversation between Luigi and his mother is also in line with Browning's tendency to keep the stage free of characters and grandiose stage effects. In each case, the encounter is between and within two people, and the only time the stage contains more than two people is in the interlude. All of this permits an intensification of internal action.

Luigi's dilemma is much like Sebald's and Jules's: his determination to act is threatened until Pippa passes. We recognize the boy's hypersensitivity from his first speech, in which he transforms wallflowers growing in the wall into a picture of political intrigue: "mountain men" and "old Franz." Luigi wants to join "the cause" of freedom against the king, but his desire is undermined by his mother. She logically argues to counter his intentions. You see only vices, she claims; and, after all, the king is old "and densely stupid." But Luigi cannot respond to reason. He is not motivated by intellectual commitment, but by his sensitivity to the political injustices which "trouble" him. By his own admission, he is not rationally responsible: "I think my mind is touched, suspect / All is not sound." "I laugh at myself," he confesses, and

> as I walk
> There's springing and melody and giddiness,
> And old quaint turns and passages of my youth,
> Dreams long forgotten, little in themselves,
> Return to me—whatever may amuse me. . . . (III.44-48)

His whole speech mirrors a mental tension finally climaxed by personification: "The very cicala laughs 'There goes he, and there!'"

The dialogue is circuitous. The mother keeps arguing on a rational level. "You never will escape," she warns. But Luigi can only respond in idealistic terms. To him, "The dying is the best part of it." Death would be a transfiguration: "I can give news of earth to all the dead / Who ask me." His vision of the world is not literal (kings, policemen, political intrigue) but poetic: "last year's sunsets, and great stars," "the crimson wave that drifts the sun away," "crescent moons," "a double rainbow," "yellow moonlit summer nights." His charged subjective state erupts in a chaotic association of images, in dreams and constant references back and forth in time.

His mother tries another means of persuasion. Your patriotism is too easily acquired, she contends: "he loves himself—and next, the world— / If he must love beyond,—but naught between." Luigi tries vainly to defend himself on political grounds. There was a false treaty, he begins,

> Or . . . better go at once to modern time,
> He has . . . they have . . . in fact, I understand
> But I can't restate the matter; that's my boast:
> Others could reason it out to you, and prove
> Things they have made me feel.   (III.141-45)

His inability to explain the situation to his mother—the stammering, the garbled syntax, the circular structure—implies that the political intrigue is more a means by which Luigi expresses his spiritual need than the primary cause for action.

Luigi's mother has one last argument, one she knows will work because it parallels her son's propensity toward dreams and visions—Chiara. She appeals to his poetic nature: "Chiara will love to see / That Jupiter an evening star next June." As she expects, Luigi picks up the vision and falls into exotic abandon:

> Great noontides, thunder-storms, all glaring pomps
> That triumph at the heels of June the god

> Leading his revel through our leafy world.
> Yes, Chiara will be here.   (III.154-57)

Just as he is caught in the ecstasy of his imagined world and loses sight of his "cause," Pippa passes and frees him from the dream.

Her song is a narrative in three parts: 1) a king lived "In the morning of the world" and, grown old, became "calm as a babe new-born," so "That, having lived thus long, there seemed / No need the king should ever die"; 2) "The king judged, sitting in the sun," the poor subjects brought to him by "angry priests"; 3) one day a deadly Python came to the city but "did not dare / Approach that threshold in the sun, / Assault the old king smiling there." Then, it seemed, kings had such grace to destroy evil. The simple parable triggers an immediate response. Now, Luigi surmises, the Python sits upon the throne, "now that the world ends! / And brave men, God would crown for slaying him, / Lurk in by-corners lest they fall his prey." It is the poetic symbol of the Python that inspires Luigi to murder the Austrian emperor, not a detailed account of political theory. " 'Tis God's call: how could I stay? Farewell!" Released from his distracting dream Luigi hears "God's call." Here, as in the other episodes, the drama ends at the moment the character commits himself to act. Political or social implications are no more important here than they are at the end of *Maud.*

The transition into the next section does more than provide a realistic backdrop for the action. It places Pippa in the specific dramatic action which is to follow. In introducing Pippa into the last episode, Browning once again struggles to fuse the overall action and the specific episodes. The Monsignor is the most imposing figure in the play and apparently Browning considered his episode the climax to the play. In addition, as critics have often noted, the play deals with levels of love, and the divine love represented by the Monsignor is the highest attainable level of love. In every respect, the play should move toward a climax in the last episode.

In the interlude a group of prostitutes express their greatest dreams, but they never exceed the everyday reality of Asolo. They wish only "This sunset / To finish," a quiet supper with a "grand-father"-lover, a "long loose gown," "milk to drink, apples to eat," "Duezans and junetings, leather coats." Each wishes a modest physical need or materialistic advance, and each is countered by harsh reality. Browning avoids sentimentalizing the workers by drawing a sharp contrast between their pragmatism and Pippa's joyous theme, between their illicit love and the divine love repre-sented by Monsignor. Apparently he wished to lessen the melo-dramatic effect of rescuing Pippa by means of her as yet undis-closed relationship to the Monsignor. He partially succeeds by enveloping Pippa in the girls' sordid ambition and consequently casting an ironic tone over the entire last scene. Pippa is no better or more noble than they, only luckier: "the great, rich handsome Englishman has fallen so violently in love" with her.

The action takes place in a room inside the palace where the Monsignor, visiting Asolo to clear up his dead brother's accounts, asks all except Ugo to leave the room. The dramatic conflict lies in the Monsignor: he knows what he must do, but his spiritual pride and sense of family honor make him prey to Ugo's devices. The mental debate sets his spiritual integrity against his pride. From the beginning, he hedges the issue of his brother's and Ugo's guilt. He discusses a letter from Jules, the sculptor now turned painter, and questions Ugo concerning the possibility that Jules may found a school like Correggio's. But his opponent sees through the dodge, "Is Correggio a painter?" He wants nothing to do with the Monsignor's digressions: "Let this farce, this chat-ter end now: what is it you want with me?" He sees "four stone walls," not the abstract Ideal the Monsignor finds in Jules's vision.

Because Ugo is an opportunist, a supreme realist, he insists that the facts be faced. He tells the Monsignor to ignore his broth-er's affairs: "They will hardly bear looking into." Ironically, be-cause he sees through the Monsignor's circumlocutions, Ugo be-comes the means of his salvation; for like Jules, the Monsignor must confess the guilt in order to be free of it. The priest first tries to escape the fact, "I would better not"; but Ugo calmly confesses that he "murdered your brother's friend, Pasquale, for him." He talks only when necessary, when his position is threatened; but the Monsignor is garrulous.

In an attempt to disassociate himself somehow from his brother's guilt, the prelate resurrects his youth as verification of his spiritual integrity: "I, the youngest, might have rivalled them in vice, if not in wealth: but from my boyhood came out from among them, and so am not partaker of their plagues." But although he claims a spiritual superiority, he cannot separate himself psychologically; to judge his brother is to judge himself. When he almost utters the condemnation of Ugo, he is interrupted by "my cough," a manifestation of his unconscious desire to conceal rather than accept his brother's guilt.

Ugo catches the implication all too clearly. The fact that the Monsignor represents the unscrupulous and wealthy church in its effort to gain the inheritance ("the Pontiff enjoins me . . . to recover it parcel by parcel, howsoever, whensoever, and wheresoever") and has not yet condemned him gives Ugo tremendous boldness: "What am I to expect? Are you going to punish me?" The priest wants to know what happened to his brother's illegitimate child. Half motivated by the desire to save Ugo's soul and half by the subconscious need to redeem the family name, he wants to know if there is a rightful heir to the villa or whether he can claim it for the church. He admits his great purpose in life has been to reclaim familial honor—"I have, I know, a chapel to support that it may rest." Now he is faced with the possibility of acquiring the villa for the church and so obliterating his brother's offenses forever.

The ambiguity of the priest's motives permits Ugo to draw his own conclusions: "The child is always ready to produce—as you say—howsoever, whensoever, wheresoever." He uses the Monsignor's own words to tempt him; and when the Monsignor offers slim resistance ("All should be sifted, however—seven times sifted"), he utters his only lengthy speech. In the discourse he clearly identifies the priest with the dark intrigues of the church and with his brother's evil: "Sir, you are no brutal dastardly idiot like your brother I frightened to death: let us understand one another." He suggests that Pippa, the bastard daughter, be sent to Rome, significantly the seat of the church, because "at Rome the courtesans perish off every three years." We receive a vivid account of the priest's response through Ugo's eyes:

> You assent, I perceive—no, that's not
> it—assent I do not say—but you will let me
> convert my present havings and holdings into
> cash, and give me time to cross the Alps?
> . . . .
> 'Tis as well settled once and forever. Some
> women I have procured will pass Bluphocks, my
> handsome scoundrel, off for somebody; and once
> Pippa entangled!—you conceive? Through her
> singing? Is it a bargain?   (IV.210-13, 218-22)

As the priest vacillates between accepting Ugo's solution to his psychological need of preserving his honor and performing his spiritual duty by sentencing him, Pippa passes.

She identifies herself as an orphan adopted by God ("Suddenly God took me in."), a representative of the poor, who suffer at the hands of people like Ugo, the Monsignor's brother, and the church itself. The priest's moral sense succumbs to Ugo's subtle persuasiveness until Pippa rejuvenates it and permits him to act. The Monsignor not only conquers the proven evil of Ugo, his brother, and the church, he temporarily saves himself from his own spiritual pride.

As Pippa reviews her day, she recognizes that "Best people are not angels quite," that even the Monsignor is a part of the flawed humanity of Asolo: "No mere mortal has a right / To carry that exalted air." And yet she condemns no one and remembers with delight her identity as each of the characters. She is at once everyone and no one. The unity of the play is her presence; but, paradoxically, she herself is only slightly more than an aspect of the major actors in the drama. Once she appears she sets the self against the self within each and therefore demands choice. However ironically, Pippa does "move them—if you please, / Do good or evil to them in some slight way."

Browning's experiment with dramatic form in *Pippa Passes* is not fully satisfying. The interior episodes do succeed (the Ottima-Sebald section brilliantly) but the exterior action does not. Browning could not resolve the enigma created by making Pippa the structural but not the dramatic locus. Whereas her experiences might be arranged chronologically from dawn to eve, the four episodes can not. For all practical purposes they exist outside time, even if the imagery within them tends to revolve around time. In that Pippa does not change in the course of her day or arrive at some point of recognition, the action, as it relates to her at least, is temporal without being progressive, that is, without moving toward a dramatic resolution. The feeble attempt to predict her future in the terminal section is more contrived than not, as though Browning felt he had to do something with her in order to end the story. Yet because she herself cannot choose her end, she stands outside the real drama. Nor does Browning manage to develop his theme climactically. If the play is structured on ascending levels of love, as seems apparent, it should reach its highest point in the last encounter dealing with the most elevated kind of love. Browning seems to have intended just that. He carefully relates Pippa to the Monsignor's brother in an obvious effort to fuse the inner and outer action. But he had already achieved an ascending pattern within the other episodes, in effect creating three separate climaxes, in contrast to the conventional single climax. Consequently, the fourth scene seems all the less dramatic and all the more anticlimactic. In fact, the Ottima-Sebald portion is such a *tour de force* that it reduces all the subsequent actions. Dramatically speaking, the problem is magnified by the difference in tone between the first and last episodes: the first begins in enormous tension because of the passionate nature of the situation, the last evolves laboriously from careful exposition and dialogue and never gains sufficient momentum. But if, as Andrea del Sarto says of Raphael Sanzio's painting, "That arm is wrongly put—and there again— / A fault to pardon in the drawing's lines, / Its body, so to speak: its soul is right."

In Browning, perhaps, we see more fully than in any other nineteenth-century English writer the dissolution of critical terminology in drama. The classical protagonist is replaced by a collective self, subdivided into several fragmented selves. The altar, the throne, the pageant give way to the sordid and common world of Asolo. If there are fundamental and ultimate values, they tend to exist in the individual rather than in the cosmos or in social law. No character measures himself or is measured by a body of beliefs outside himself. With the disappearance of social and moral law, the individual assumes total responsibility for his acts and sits in judgment of himself. No plagues are lifted, no kings crowned. It is no accident that Browning admired Euripides more than the earlier Greek dramatists because he found in him some of the same awareness of the effect of social disorder upon character that he himself examined: "Because Euripides shrank not to teach, / If gods be strong and wicked, man, though weak, / May prove their match by willing to be good" ("Aristophanes' Apology"). Aristotle could not have served him so well.

According to Clement Tyson Goode, "English drama received a new impulse, a new inspiration, a new lease of life, and withal a new idea of what was possible for it, almost immediately after Byron."[19] But what did follow Byron? Comedy was replaced by spectacles, as the popularity of James Robinson Planché affirms. Farces, burlesques, and comic operas replaced serious drama. Romantic tragedy held the boards at least until Browning's *A Blot in the 'Scutcheon*. The Gothic tradition was carried on by Planché and Edward Fitzball, among others. Douglas William Jerrold and Fitzball developed the English nautical melodrama. Jerrold in turn domesticated the drama and turned to more native English settings. Then came the French influence; by the time Browning was writing Bulwer-Lytton was adhering to French forms in his highly successful domestic dramas. And a year after *Strafford* was finished, Dion Boucicault began his career and continued the tradition of the "well-made" play on both the British and American stages. Surely if Browning entered a "new" theater in the late 1830s and 1840s, it was not a better theater. Where in England would he have seen a play like *Pippa* produced?

Pippa, concludes James McCormick, "was a sword, one that Bulwer-Lytton could not fashion but one that Robert Browning and some twentieth-century playwrights could forge." Browning was bound to fail, he goes on to say, because it was not until the Moscow Art Theatre was born fifty-eight years later in 1898 that a theater existed "capable of interpreting the fluid movement of his play."[20]

Every imaginative dramatist is limited by the stage tradition in his own age, perhaps, but nineteenth-century writers faced a more severe problem than most. Shakespeare may not have had the physical facilities of a modern stage, but he had a vibrant native tradition behind him. The ritual and pageantry of the medieval stage; the mighty line, the hero, and the dramatic effects developed in the Marlovian drama; the refinements of numerous other pioneers in drama; all of these gave to Shakespeare resources denied nineteenth-century poets. For Browning, there were no playwrights to follow, no stage traditions suited to his purpose, and no theaters to test out his theories before a sympathetic audience. Had he been aware of the possibilities of a modern stage, had he, for example, observed Chekhov's ensemble dramatic style or Stanislavsky's methodology, he might have found some means other than the spoken word of conveying "Action in Character." Had he had the opportunity to do it again for a more modern stage, as he himself admitted near the end of his life, he would have written more for an audience "all eyes" than "all ears."[21] But given the limitation of the stage at mid-century and, above all, the inaccessibility of viable stage models, Browning, like Byron, could turn only to a mental theater with an imaginary stage and an unseen audience.

5

END AND BEGINNING

> The change from traditional literature . . . can be defined as a
> moving of once objective worlds of myth and romance into
> the subjective consciousness of man.
>
> J. HILLIS MILLER,*The Disappearance of God*

The miscarriage of serious drama in the nineteenth century was
the price paid for experimentation with form. The death knell of
classical tragedy had already sounded before the romantic poets
took to the stage.[1] A vague resemblance to the architectonic design of Greek tragedy lingered in the syllogistic "myth of order"
of Racine's baroque dramas, but when he died in 1699 no one
remained worthy of the name tragedian. With the publication of
Lillo's *The London Merchant* in 1731 tragedy ceased to be a functional term—comparisons between classical tragedy and the bour-
geois tragedies of the eighteenth century are ludicrous nonsense.
For nearly a century banal melodramas ruled the boards, save for
the brief respite of Sheridan's comedies. Then Goethe wrote
Faust. The quest for a modern drama had begun:

> Goethe was the first to discard everything external as unim-
> portant: with him drama enters the realm of psychological
> experience, with the hero suffering a spiritual development,
> or rather crisis. . . . This tendency to lay the main stress on

psychological analysis, whether the characters analyse themselves or are exposed to the shrewd observations of other characters in the dialogue, later becomes so significant for modern drama that we forget that it did not occur, for instance, in Elizabethan drama.[2]

If Goethe initiated a new drama, he hardly determined it. The transformation of dramatic form became a program of Continental writers. Hugo called for a new drama born of "a new religion, a new society." Hebbel envisioned a new dialectical structure in drama between protagonist and "Idea." Nietzsche announced the birth of a new tragedy just two years before Zola rejected all formulas, standards and traditions in the Preface to *Thérèse Raquin*. About the same time Wagner urged an almost total assertion of will over intellect in *Ueber die Bestimmung der Oper*. By the end of the century Strindberg and Ibsen wrestled with the apparently opposing forces of psychological realism and aesthetic form. Chekhov examined the possibilities of a drama virtually without plot. Then too, there were unrecognized rebels in the revolution. In 1837 Georg Büchner wrote *Woyzeck*, a play remarkable in its modern content and form. Breaking from all known or accepted dramatic formulas, he examined the effects of psychological determinism on character in a collection of two dozen brief expressionistic scenes. In England a silent revolution was also taking place. Though lacking a declaration of independence such as that provided for poetry in the Preface to *Lyrical Ballads*, Shelley, Byron, Browning, and Tennyson groped toward a modern drama.

Though much like the popular plays of the time in Elizabethan format, Shelley's *The Cenci* lacks the geometric proportion of Renaissance drama. Plot is less the end than the catalyst of action, less the structural center than a visual means of portraying the conflict within Beatrice. However unknowingly, Shelley inverts Shakespearean dramaturgy. M. C. Bradbrook contends that *King Lear* "seems to speak more clearly to our condition than any other of Shakespeare's plays."[3] Perhaps so, but *Lear* is not yet modern drama. It describes in tragic rhythm the destruction of a king who sins against the moral and ethical code; *The Cenci* records the destruction of one who expresses full conviction in a code no longer valid. The "tragedy" is not that man has fallen from grace, but that he remains in perpetual uncertainty and incompleteness. Beatrice seeks commitment in a world in which commitment is impossible. In *Lear* ritual fulfills the need for unity; in *The Cenci* the modulations of Beatrice's mind chart an ambiguous course. Admittedly the Gothic plot sometimes shrouds the matrix of the action, or the struggle of will within Beatrice; nevertheless, in spite of Shelley's ignorance of the stage and unawareness of the structural difficulties in the play, *The Cenci* is a landmark in English drama. Its hybrid form exposes the differences between modern and traditional drama and the inappropriateness of classical form to modern subjective matter.

Byron's *Cain* divorces itself more overtly from dramatic conventions. Alienated from the stage—partly by intent, to be sure —Byron followed Goethe's lead and developed an early antihero for the drama. As part of his experiment to found a "mental theatre," Byron replaces plot with internal debate as the basis of action in *Cain*. Cain's isolation affirms an intellectual independence. Rather than being the agent in the inevitable ritual of tragic action, he assumes autonomy in his defiance of the cosmic and social orientation of his world. In many ways he anticipates what Robert Brustein calls the messianic hero in the modern "theatre of revolt." "Messianic drama," Brustein argues, "is a medium of absolute liberation, unrestrained by dramatic rules or human limitations, through which the rebel dramatist indulges his insatiable appetite for the infinite."[4] In a sense the superhumanity of Cain sweeps away all external judgments. If he is evil, his evil is paradoxically his good. Like Strindberg's Stranger (who claims, "I am Cain, you see."), he acquires his power from the total rejection of anything outside self. Granting that Byron exaggerates Cain's virtue and diminishes God to the level of petty tyrant, he nonetheless introduces a distinctly modern hero to English drama. His experiments with dramatic form, his attempt to place the drama within the mind, and his abandonment of conventional stage setting prove that he sensed the need of liberation from orthodox drama.

Browning resembles more a modern existentialist dramatist than a "messianic" one. In seeking a "Pit-audience" sympathetic with his preoccupation with "incidents in the development of a soul," Browning came "full circle from the Aristotelian literature of action—from a deductive literature where character is a deviation from the Truth which action restores, to an inductive literature where action is the experience through which character creates at least one possible truth. . . ."[5] The limited episodes of *Pippa Passes* with their restricted setting and concentration on characters at a moment of climax throw full focus on subjective action. Judged by traditional standards, *Pippa Passes* fails utterly; judged as an experiment to objectify subjective matter, it is a genuine achievement. Browning's use of dialogue, setting, and limited stage action anticipates both the realism and symbolism of a later period. The episodic structure cancels out plot as the "soul of action" and frees character from subservience to it. Much like the modern existentialist, Browning recognized that the conflict between stasis and action, between negation (sensual love in the Ottima-Sebald episode, a faraway isle in the Jules-Phene episode, Chiara in the Luigi-Mother episode, Uguccio's offer in the last episode) and affirmation can be resolved only by an assertion of will. In *Pippa* we discover not faith but "the varieties of religious experience" and the single religion of the self. "What man wants is simply independent choice," says Dostoevsky's underground man, "whatever that independence may cost and wherever it may lead. And choice, of course, the devil knows what choice. . . ."[6] Although lacking a playable form, *Pippa* develops dramatic techniques far in advance of other nineteenth-century plays. It is expressionistic and realistic at the same time. If its publication offered no stage model for other dramatists to imitate, it attests that Browning, at least, recognized the need for a new construct.

The ritual of modern drama is often the anticipatory pattern of psychological manifestations emanating from character rather than the ritual of ethical order in which the hero is placed. *Maud's* modernity is in the synthesis of psychological realism and aesthetic form. If Hamlet "is the prisoner of a police system,"[7] *Maud's* lover is a prisoner of his own consciousness. If ghosts in Shakespeare are visitors from another world, in *Maud* they are a psychic reality (they are both a biological and psychic reality in Ibsen's *Ghosts*). If Hamlet's supposed madness is played out in a fixed ethical framework, if Lear's madness reveals world chaos as the wages of sin, the derangement of *Maud's* lover reveals the effects of psychic sickness. We receive no profound insights into the loss of values in the world at large in *Maud*, but we witness one "soul's" efforts to resurrect itself in an inner world of decadence and morbidity. Tennyson's work is at least a precursor of modern concepts of dramatic action. It is a poem, but it is also a blatantly subjective dramatic piece. Limited by the drama of his day, Tennyson could not envision in the 1850s a stage capable of producing *Maud*. Though he considered it a monodrama, he forgot the stage in order to concentrate on the revelation of character through language and symbol, through a medley of figures and images in the speaker's mind. Nevertheless, *Maud* belongs in a discussion of drama, because it foreshadows the works of early modern dramatists. Grotesque figures and fantasies such as those who torment Strindberg's heroes intrude upon the narrator's degenerate mind. Like Strindberg and Ibsen, Tennyson explores the deepest regions of the mind through metaphor and symbol. Because he lacked stage knowledge and a stage model, he depended on the poetic medium rather than dramatic incident and staging, but the dramatic conception of *Maud* is clearly akin to the preoccupation with internal reality in early modern drama.

In *Beatrice Cenci*, in *Cain*, in Browning's heroes, and *Maud's* lover, we witness the destruction and partial resurrection of the self in a world already ineffectual. J. Hillis Miller discusses this change as the "transformation of the objective fact, God," into a "figment of man's imagination":

> The ideal world still exists, but only as a form of consciousness, not as an objective fact. The drama has all been moved

within the minds of the characters, and the world as it is in itself is by implication unattainable or of no consequence. Love, honor, God himself exist, but only because someone believes in them. And as soon as a man sees God in this way he is effectively cut off from the living God of faith.[8]

Nineteenth-century writers were aware of their spiritual crisis, as their poetry richly attests. They brought to the drama this same awareness; and, deprived of a suitable form to replace the now inappropriate ritual of classical drama, they sought an objective expression for their feelings of despair. They sensed, if they did not fully express, the death of tragedy.

Their dramas suggest that with the evaporation of socially defined values and myths, the old drama could not survive. Nietzsche predicted that when God is dead, tragic poetry will cease to exist. Strip away the heavens and all signs of the mysterious transcendent power at work in the universe—sometimes appearing as God, nature, fate, society—and leave only man, suffering punishment and enjoying reward solely by his own hand, and modern drama is born. The symbols of the communal order disappear, and "man finds himself alone and in spiritual poverty." Man's reflex action, concludes J. Hillis Miller, is "withdrawal into the privacy of consciousness."[9] The individual has strayed so far from a communal order in our own age that Eric Bentley has warned, "If a man claims to have discovered the mythos of the twentieth century we know he is a charlatan and we suspect that he is well paid for it."[10] If he is right in observing the dichotomy between art and the popular stage in our age, then surely the impulse of major nineteenth-century writers was equally accurate.

Shelley, Byron, Tennyson, and Browning did not produce a new dramatic system even though they experimented with dramatic form. Allardyce Nicoll is correct in this assumption at least: "not one produced a dramatic masterpiece which can be looked upon as the starting-point for further art development."[11] But major writers knew instinctively that drama would never be the same again. In England the aesthetic revolution and the really innovative efforts of the age were assigned to an empty or deserted stage. Indeed, only when the stage was deserted, emptied of sets used superficially and emptied of actions used merely to advance a story, only then could subjective drama occur in which the hero created the set and characters which mirror his inner states and conflicts.

Matthew Arnold, whose sense of history allowed him to feel more deeply than most the full weight of the modern condition, knew well enough where the difficulty lay:

> The confusion of the present time is great, the multitude of voices counselling differing things bewildering, the number of exciting works capable of attracting a young writer's attention and of becoming his models, immense: what he wants is a hand to guide him through the confusion, a voice to prescribe to him the aim which he should keep in view, and to explain to him that the value of the literary works which offer themselves to his attention is relative to their power of helping him forward on his road towards this end. Such a guide the English writer at the present day will nowhere find.[12]

Nor is modern drama likely to establish one dramatic mode. The uniformity of classical drama is impossible in a pluralistic society. There is no longer the inevitable relationship between audience and artist. In fact, one of the major drives in modern literature is the compulsion to find or even to cultivate an audience. The disappearance of poetic drama, symptomatic of the breakdown of a common language between audience and artist in the theater, is clearly a fact. The "poetry" of chaos, the grotesque imagery and violent language of the current stage, has become the dialogue of modern drama. An age of flux denies a drama of stability and faith. If mythic figures have reappeared, they are visible only in the post-Freudian garb of O'Neill's heroes, the Jungian archetypes of Yeats, or the antiheroes of Anouilh, Giraudoux, Sartre, and Cocteau. There is no longer *the* drama, but a drama characterized by dissimilarity and unending change. Still the search for dramatic form initiated in the nineteenth century continues. Serious nineteenth-century English poets were participants in that quest.

NOTES

Notes to Introduction

1. See Allardyce Nicoll, *A History of English Drama, 1660-1900*, 2d ed. (Cambridge: At the University Press, 1959), vol. 4, *Early Nineteenth Century Drama, 1800-1850*; George Rowell, *The Victorian Theatre: A Survey* (London: Oxford University Press, 1956); and George Steiner, *The Death of Tragedy* (London: Faber and Faber, 1961), especially pp. 110-21. Other important studies include Ernest B. Watson, *Sheridan to Robertson: A Study of the Nineteenth-Century English Stage* (Cambridge, Mass.: Harvard University Press, 1926); U. C. Nag, "The English Theater of the Romantic Revival," *The Nineteenth Century and After* 104 (1928): 384-98; Richard M. Fletcher, *English Romantic Drama, 1795-1843: A Critical History* (New York: Exposition Press, Inc., 1966); John W. Ehrstine, "The Drama and Romantic Theory: The Cloudy Symbols of High Romance," *Research Studies* 34 (1966): 85-106.

2. See especially Morse Peckham, *Beyond the Tragic Vision: The Quest for Identity in the Nineteenth Century* (New York: George Braziller, Inc., 1962); J. Hillis Miller, *The Disappearance of God: Five Nineteenth-Century Writers* (Cambridge, Mass.: Harvard University Press, 1963); Robert Langbaum, *The Poetry of Experience: The Dramatic Monologue in Modern Literary Tradition* (New York: Random House, Inc.; London: Chatto & Windus, Ltd., 1957); M. H. Abrams, *The Mirror and the Lamp: The Romantic Theory and the Critical Tradition* (New York: Oxford University Press, 1953); Northrop Frye, *A Study of English Romanticism* (New York: Random House, Inc., 1968), chap. 1, "The Romantic Myth," pp. 3-49.

3. *A Course of Lectures on Dramatic Art and Literature*, trans. John Black, 2d ed. (London: J. Templeman; J. R. Smith, 1840), 2:102. Modern German dramatic criticism dates from 1776 when Lessing was named the critic of the New National Theatre in Hamburg. The Schlegels, Goethe, and such later critics as Otto Ludwig and Friedrich Hebbel produced a substantial body of criticism for the new drama.

4. Ibid., 1:340. Elsewhere in the same lecture Schlegel notes that Aristotle "understands by *action* . . . merely something that takes place."

5. *The Poetry of Experience*, p. 227.

6. *Shakespeare: The Complete Works*, ed. G. B. Harrison (New York: Harcourt, Brace & World, Inc., 1952), p. 83. It is indicative that Bradley could add a lengthy note devoted to the question of where Hamlet was dur-

Notes

ing his father's funeral. Harrison's summary of "Romantic criticism" of Shakespeare is pithy but inclusive. See also, Robert Fricker, "Shakespeare und das Englische Romantische Drama," *Shakespeare Jahrbuch* 95 (1959): 63-81; and Helmut Viebrock, "Shakespeare und die Englische Romantik," *Shakespeare Jahrbuch* 97 (1961): 34-62.

7. *Mimesis: The Representation of Reality in Western Literature*, trans. Willard Trask (Garden City, N. Y.: Doubleday & Co., Inc., 1953; first published in Berne, Switzerland, 1946), p. 285. "Once we lose sight of the worldview out of which [Greek] plays were written," Langbaum writes, "we read them psychologically as we have done with Shakespeare. In other words, we reverse Aristotle by giving the primacy to character over action. For the whole Aristotelian analysis . . . breaks down once we regard the characters as, in a democratic sense, people rather than as hierarchical categories of people" (p. 221).

8. Recorded in memoranda of Henry Holgate Carwardine, first published in *Notes and Queries*, 2 April, 1870.

9. Walter Jackson Bate, *From Classic to Romantic: Premises of Taste in Eighteenth Century England* (1946; reprint ed., New York: Harper & Row, Pubs., 1961), p. 16. Nor could the eighteenth-century drama of sensibility provide a suitable model for the new drama. It was founded on an absolute confidence in man's goodness as the logical manifestation of universal order. In modern drama the ethos is shattered: man's superiority is no longer guaranteed by the immutable laws of a benevolent cosmic order, nor is his perfectability deemed possible. See Ernest Bernbaum, *The Drama of Sensibility: A Sketch of the History of Sentimental and Domestic Tragedy, 1696-1780* (1915; reprint ed., Gloucester, Mass.: Peter Smith, 1958) for a discussion of early "dramas of feeling."

10. *Rousseau and Romanticism*, 5th ed. (New York: Meridian Books, 1960), p. 16.

11. *Friedrich Schlegel, 1794-1802. Seine Prosaischen Jugendschriften*, ed. J. Minor (Vienna: Verlagsbuchhandlung Carl Konegen, 1906), 1:171. The conflict between subjective matter and objective form in nineteenth-century literature has been the subject of numerous studies. As pertains to drama, the best recent discussion is to be found in Patricia Ball's book, *The Central Self: A Study in Romantic and Victorian Imagination* (London: Athlone Press, 1968), chap. 2, "The Romantics as Dramatists," pp. 22-63. "In each branch of their work," she writes, "a chameleon activity coexists with egotistical. First, in the plays, where orthodox chameleon activity is inherent in the form, the expected 'Shakespearean' qualities . . . are crossed with the egotistical tendency and with the peculiarly Romantic significance of the chameleon itself. . . . They emerge as central efforts of the Romantic imagination, not peripheral mistakes" (p. 22).

12. Langbaum, *The Poetry of Experience*, r 20.

13. J. O. Bailey, *British Plays of the Nineteenth Century: An Anthology to Illustrate the Evolution of the Drama* (New York: Odyssey Press, 1966), p. 23.

Notes to Chapter 1

1. (1947; reprint ed., Bloomington: Indiana University Press, 1966), p. 244.

2. *The Complete Works of Percy Bysshe Shelley*, ed. Roger Ingpen and

Walter E. Peck (New York: Charles Scribner's Sons, 1926-1930), 10:73 (hereafter cited as *Works*).

3. Throughout I have used the Hutchinson edition of *The Cenci* complete with the preface and Mary Shelley's notes (*The Complete Works of Percy Bysshe Shelley*, ed. Thomas Hutchinson [1905; reprint ed., New York: Oxford University Press, 1951]).

4. *The Life of Percy Bysshe Shelley as Comprised in The Life of Shelley by Thomas Jefferson Hogg. The Recollections of Shelley and Byron by Edward John Trelawny. Memoirs of Shelley by Thomas Love Peacock*, ed. Humbert Wolfe (New York: E. P. Dutton & Co., Inc., 1933), 2:330.

5. *Trelawny*, 2:198.

6. *Peacock*, 2:330.

7. *The Nascent Mind of Shelley* (Oxford: Clarendon Press, 1947), p. 260.

8. *Shelley: A Life Story* (1946; reprint ed., New York: Viking Press, Inc., 1965), p. 193.

9. (Albuquerque: University of New Mexico Press, 1967), p. 194.

10. *Trelawny*, 2:198.

11. *A Study of English Romanticism*, p. 47.

12. Moody Prior is representative of the first group of critics. For him the center of action is "the grim opposition . . . the essential conflict, the terrible struggle between Cenci and Beatrice." This conflict, he contends, is depicted by the imagery of dark and light: "on the one hand the dark, violent, corrupt, satanic; on the other, beauty, light, quiet strength" (*The Language of Tragedy*, pp. 228, 232). William Marshall has explained the reason for the play's apparent disunity: "Though the elements of the story imply that we should move intellectually in one direction, the force of the personality of the central character, consistently sustained despite the ethical confusion, moves us in quite another" (*"Caleb Williams* and *The Cenci,"* *Notes and Queries*, no. 7 [1960], p. 263). And Joseph W. Donohue, Jr., has offered the ingenious suggestion that Shelley creates two Beatrices: "one who exists in a hypothetical life outside the events of the story, the other, a 'dramatic counter' whose fundamental nature derives from the act she commits under extraordinary duress . . ." ("Shelley's Beatrice and the Romantic Concept of Tragic Character," *Keats-Shelley Journal* 17 [1968]: 54).

13. The most extensive treatment of the play is Stuart Curran's excellent study, *Shelley's Cenci: Scorpions Ringed with Fire* (Princeton: Princeton University Press, 1970). His examination of "the meaning, the range and the influence" of *The Cenci* greatly supersedes the much earlier book devoted to the play, Ernest Sutherland Bates's *A Study of Shelley's Drama The Cenci* (New York: Columbia University Press, 1908). See also, Benjamin P. Kurtz, *The Pursuit of Death: A Study of Shelley's Poetry* (London: Oxford University Press, 1933), pp. 190-201; Milton Thomas Wilson, *Shelley's Later Poetry: A Study of his Prophetic Imagination* (New York: Columbia University Press, 1959), pp. 78-92; Desmond King-Hele, *Shelley: The Man and the Poet* (New York: Thomas Yoseloff, Inc., 1960), pp. 118-38; Charles L. Adams, "The Structure of *The Cenci," Drama Survey* 4 (1965): 139-48; James Rieger, *The Mutiny Within: The Heresies of Percy Bysshe Shelley* (New York: George Braziller, Inc., 1967), pp. 111-21; Truman G. Steffan, "Seven Accounts of *The Cenci* and Shelley's Drama," *Studies in English Literature* 9 (1969): 601-18.

14. (New York: New York University Press, 1969), p. 11. See Stuart Curran's illuminating discussion of the "profoundly sexual and profoundly metaphysical" incestuous act (*Shelley's Cenci*, esp. pp. 136-54).

15. For a sensitive treatment of the passage see Richard Harter Fogle, *The Imagery of Keats and Shelley* (Chapel Hill: University of North Carolina Press, 1949), pp. 180-82.

16. See Robert F. Whitman, "Beatrice's 'Pernicious Mistake' in *The Cenci*," *PMLA* 74 (1959): 249-53.

17. Newman Ivey White notes that by the time Shelley was writing *The Cenci* he was "quite clear that the seat of evil was in man himself, and not primarily in the evil institutions that were merely the result of that fact" (*Shelley* [New York: Alfred A. Knopf, Inc., 1940], 2:144). Joseph Barrell similarly argues that late in his life Shelley "gained the conviction from Plato that the responsibility for evil is clearly made to rest on man himself" (*Shelley and the Thought of his Time* [New Haven: Yale University Press, 1947], p. 141). C. S. Lewis refers to *The Revolt of Isam*, *Prometheus Unbound*, and *The Triumph of Life* to prove his thesis that "It is simply not true to say that Shelley conceives the human Soul as a naturally innocent and divinely beautiful creature, interfered with by external tyrants. . . . no other heathen writer comes nearer to stating and driving home the doctrine of original sin" (from *Rehabilitations and Other Essays*, reprinted in *English Romantic Poets: Modern Essays in Criticism*, ed. M. H. Abrams [New York: Oxford University Press, 1960], p. 256). Stuart Curran's comments on Shelley's concept of good and evil are especially revealing (*Shelley's Cenci*, pp. 129-54).

18. *The Disappearance of God*, p. 7.

19. See especially Carl Grabo, *The Magic Plant: The Growth of Shelley's Thought* (Chapel Hill: University of North Carolina Press, 1936), pp. 299-304; Carlos Baker, *Shelley's Major Poetry: The Fabric of a Vision* (1948; reprint ed., New York: Russell and Russell, Pubs., 1961), pp. 142-53; Whitman, "Beatrice's 'Mistake,'" pp. 250-53; Curran, *Shelley's Cenci*, pp. 136-54. It should be remembered that Shelley was working on *Prometheus Unbound* when he wrote *The Cenci*. In fact he stopped work on *Prometheus* for a period of two months after having written three acts in order to write the entire *Cenci*. Barrell makes the important observation that when Shelley returned to *Prometheus* he altered his purpose. The Greek emphasis on thought gave way in the fourth act to Shelley's belief that feeling "should be given the chief place in the world." Rather than achieving the metaphysical resolve possible in Greek drama, Barrell adds, Shelley all but rejected the idea of a static order and let Demogorgon allow "evil as a positive force to rise again in the world" (*Shelley and the Thought of his Time*, pp. 157-60).

20. *The Complete Plays of Henry James*, ed. Leon Edel (Philadelphia: J. P. Lippincott Co., 1949), p. 53.

21. Stuart Curran shows just how modern Shelley's dramatic vision is by comparing *The Cenci* to several twentieth-century dramas; see especially *Shelley's Cenci*, pp. 277-82.

Notes to Chapter 2

1. *The Death of Tragedy*, pp. 201-2.

2. *The Works of Lord Byron. Letters and Journals*, ed. Rowland Prothero, rev. ed. (London: John Murray Co., 1902), 2: 145-55, 156-61, 166-70. Hereafter referred to as *L & J*.

3. *Byron: The Poet* (London: Gollancz, 1964), p. 107.

4. Byron wrote John Murray on August 23, 1821, "my dramatic sim-

plicity is *studiously* Greek, and must continue so: no reform ever succeeded at first. I admire the old English dramatists; but this is quite another field, and has nothing to do with theirs. I want to make a *regular* English drama, no matter whether for the stage or not, which is not my object—but a *mental theatre*." *L&J* 5: 347.

5. Throughout I use the following edition of *Cain*: Truman Guy Steffan, *Lord Byron's Cain: Twelve Essays and a Text with Variants and Annotations* (Austin: University of Texas Press, 1968).

6. References to *Manfred* and *Werner* are from *The Works of Lord Byron. Poetry*, ed. Ernest Hartley Coleridge, rev. ed. (London: John Murray Co., 1901), vols. 4 and 5.

7. *Anatomy of Criticism: Four Essays* (Princeton: Princeton University Press, 1957), p. 207.

8. *The Poetry of Experience*, p. 68.

9. "I have gone upon the notion of Cuvier, that the world has been destroyed three or four times, and was inhabited by mammoths, behemoths, and what not; but *not* by man till the Mosaic period. . . . I have, therefore, supposed Cain to be shown, in the *rational* Preadamites, beings endowed with a higher intelligence than man, but totally unlike him in form, and with much greater strength of mind and person" (Byron to Thomas Moore, 19 September 1821, *L & J* 5:368).

10. *The Romantic Ventriloquists: Wordsworth, Coleridge, Keats, Shelley, Byron* (Seattle: University of Washington Press, 1963), p. 286.

11. *The Visionary Company: A Reading of English Romantic Poetry* (Garden City, N. Y.: Doubleday & Co., Inc., 1961), p. 246.

12. *The Structure of Byron's Major Poetry* (Philadelphia: University of Pennsylvania Press, 1962), p. 140.

13. "Byron's *Cain*," *PMLA* 84 (1969): 71. Michaels's whole discussion of the ironic "concentration on the form of the form . . . in order to emphasize the extraordinary consciousness of the hero" is an excellent criticism of the play.

14. *Naturalism in English Poetry* (New York: E. P. Dutton & Co., Inc., 1920), p. 284.

15. *The Dramas of Lord Byron: A Critical Study* (1915; reprint ed., New York: Russell and Russell, Pubs., 1964), p. 55.

16. *Beyond the Tragic Vision*, p. 370. In discussing Goethe's *Faust* Erich Heller has concluded, "His 'tragedy' is that he is incapable of tragedy. For tragedy presupposes the belief in an external order of things which is indeed incomplete without the conformity of the human soul, but would be still more defective without the soul's freedom to violate it. Yet Faust's dilemma is different. His 'two souls' are merely the one soul divided in itself because it knows of no independent external reality to which it is related as a free agent" (*The Disinherited Mind* [New York: Meridian Books, 1965], p. 60).

17. *Lord Byron's Correspondence*, ed. John Murray (New York: Charles Scribner's Sons, 1922), 2:201-2.

18. See T. H. Vail Motter, "Byron's *Werner* Re-estimated: A Neglected Chapter in Nineteenth Century Stage History," in *The Parrott Presentation Volume*, ed. Hardin Craig (Princeton: Princeton University Press, 1935).

19. *Lord Byron: un tempérament littéraire* (Paris: Le Cercle Du Livre, 1957), p. 189.

20. *Byron: The Poet*, p. 125.

21. "Byron's Stage Fright: The History of his Ambition and Fear of Writing for the Stage," *ELH* 6 (1939): 242.

22. *Jeffrey's Literary Criticism*, ed. D. Nichol Smith (London: Humphrey Milford, 1928), p. 167.

23. Steiner, *The Death of Tragedy*, p. 202. According to Donald Hassler, *Marino Faliero* fails because the hero's style is inappropriate to his revolutionary ideas ("*Marino Faliero*, The Byronic Hero, and *Don Juan*," *Keats-Shelley Journal* 14 [1965]: 55-64).

24. *The Pilgrim of Eternity: Byron—A Conflict* (New York: George H. Doran Co., 1925), p. 313.

25. *Rousseau and Romanticism*, p. 165.

26. Escarpit, *Lord Byron*, p. 192.

27. *The Theatre of Revolt: An Approach to the Modern Drama* (Boston: Little, Brown and Co., 1964), p. 4.

Notes to Chapter 3

1. The quotation is from Edmund Wilson, *Axel's Castle: A Study in the Imaginative Literature of 1870-1930* (1931; reprint ed., New York: Charles Scribner's Sons, 1959), pp. 21-22. For a statement on the close relation between *Maud* and the symbolist tradition in poetry, see especially E. D. H. Johnson, "The Lily and the Rose: Symbolic Meaning in Tennyson's 'Maud,'" *PMLA* 64 (1949): 1222-27.

2. Hallam Lord Tennyson, *Alfred Lord Tennyson: A Memoir by his Son* (New York: The Macmillan Co., 1911), 2:151 (hereafter cited as *Memoir*). Tennyson's calling *Maud* a "little *Hamlet*" resulted in the inevitable reaction of early critics. I'Anson Fausset pointed out the obvious nobility and intelligence of Hamlet in contrast to the "erotomaniac" hero of *Maud* and concluded that "the soul, of which 'Maud' is claimed to be a drama, is almost entirely absent from the poem. It is sensational melodrama, containing a number of exquisitely sentimental songs, to display, as it were, the high notes of the hero's tenor voice" (*Tennyson: A Modern Portrait* [New York: D. Appleton and Co., 1923], pp. 193-94). Elisabeth L. Cary reached a similar conclusion and added, "It is easy to pity him, but the sense of illimitable tragedy is wanting, since there is no indication that in the best of health he would have been other than an ineffectual, gelatinous sort of person" (*Tennyson: His Homes, His Friends, and His Works* [New York: G. P. Putnam's Sons, 1898], p. 154). Tennyson himself wrote to Gerald Massey that he was not "comparing poor little 'Maud' to the Prince, except as, what's the old quotation out of Virgil, 'sic parvis pomponere, etc.'" (*Memoir* 1: 406). See also, Thomas P. Harrison, "Tennyson's *Maud* and Shakespeare," *Shakespeare Association Bulletin* 17 (1942): 80-85.

3. Roy P. Basler argues a strong case for Tennyson "as psychologist." He contends that Tennyson "was remarkably familiar with the phenomena of irrational as well as rational mental behavior, and that as artist he undertook to use them realistically in developing his theme" ("Tennyson the Psychologist," *South Atlantic Quarterly* 43 [1944]: 144). Basler's whole article, though restricted, is a provocative reading of the psychological motivations which dictate the structure of *Maud*. The best single essay on the poem as a whole is Clyde de L. Ryals's, "Tennyson's 'Maud,'" *Connotation* 1 (1962): 12-32. Ryals's approach is particularly valuable in placing Maud in the mainstream of early modern poetry. He offers an illuminating comparison of *Maud* and Eliot's *The Waste Land*.

4. Ronald Peacock uses this phrase in discussing "The Eve of St. Agnes" in *The Art of Drama* (London: Routledge and Kegan Paul, 1957), p. 20.

5. I have used the Hallam Tennyson edition of Tennyson's works throughout. *The Works of Alfred Lord Tennyson*, ed. Hallam Lord Tennyson, 6 vols. (London: Macmillan & Co., 1908).

6. The sound and imagery in the poem are discussed thoroughly in two excellent essays: Edward Stokes, "The Metrics of *Maud*," *Victorian Poetry* 2 (1964): 97-110; John Killham, "Tennyson's *Maud*—The Function of the Imagery," in *Critical Essays on the Poetry of Tennyson*, ed. John Killham (London: Routledge and Kegan Paul, 1960), pp. 210-35.

7. *Tennyson's Maud: The Biographical Genesis* (Berkeley and Los Angles: University of California Press, 1964), p. 108.

8. Many critics consider the ending inappropriate or ineffectual. John W. Cunliffe mistakenly assumes that Tennyson intended the war as a final solution and complains that the hero's "complete nervous equilibrium at the end of the poem" is incredulous after we see him in the first of the poem "as a neurotic . . . passing through a phase of mania" (*Leaders of the Victorian Revolution* [New York: D. Appleton-Century Co., 1943], p. 135). Humbert Wolfe suggests that the poem should have concluded at the end of Part 1, but he says that Tennyson thought "the poem . . . needed its three periods—darkness, night, and then the recurrent dark in full fugue" (*Tennyson* [London: Faber and Faber, 1930], p. 44). E. D. H. Johnson calls the ending simply "a sop to Victorian sentimentalism" and misses the significance of the war in the dramatic action (*The Alien Vision of Victorian Poetry: Sources of the Poetic Imagination in Tennyson, Browning, and Arnold* [Princeton: Princeton University Press, 1952], p. 31). Paull Baum labels *Maud* "a child of the Crimean War" and reads the poem inaccurately as basically an expression of Tennyson's concern with the war (*Tennyson Sixty Years After* [Chapel Hill: University of North Carolina Press, 1948], p. 134). Valerie Pitt reads *Maud* as Tennyson's "central political poem" and claims that "*Maud's* hero . . . sets an example" in going to war (*Tennyson Laureate* [Toronto: University of Toronto Press, 1963], p. 180). Jerome Buckley is more accurate when he calls the war "a 'moral equivalent' for the immoral war within" (*Tennyson: The Growth of a Poet* [Cambridge, Mass.: Harvard University Press, 1960], p. 142). Roy Basler ("Tennyson the Psychologist," p. 154) comes closer to the truth when he points out that the hero cannot be "completely cured of psychic illness" by the war. He "has merely exchanged one obsession, self-destruction, for another, self-sacrifice in a noble cause." Nevertheless, we might add, the action permitted by the war is the only means of salvation open to the hero. See also Patricia Ball's argument that "the hero is only released from his nightmare by his discovery that participating in the world of others can re-establish a more tolerable sense of his own identity" (*The Central Self*, pp. 180-81).

9. *The Poetry of Experience*, p. 158. "For me the instant of choice is very serious," Kierkegaard said, "because there is danger afoot, danger that the next instant it may not be equally in my power to choose, that something already has been lived which must be lived over again" (*Either/Or*, trans. Walter Lowrie [1944; reprint ed., Garden City, N. Y.: Doubleday & Co., Inc., 1959], 2:168).

10. The phrase is from Peacock, *The Art of Drama*, p. 158.

11. "From 1869 to 1880 my brother, myself and the younger members of the Cameron family spent many of our evenings during the Christmas and Easter holidays in Mrs. Cameron's little theatre. Here we acted plays by Sheridan, Gilbert, Robertson and Tom Taylor, and my father was seldom absent, for he loved the stage" (*Memoir* 2:84-85).

12. *Tennyson Sixty Years After*, p. 214.

Notes

13. Ibid., p. 220.
14. "Robert Browning and the Experimental Drama," *PMLA* 68 (1953): 986-87.
15. *The Victorian Theatre*, pp. 95-97.
16. The passages are from Irving's two addresses entitled "The Art of Acting" delivered at Harvard University in 1885 and at the Philosophical Institution at Edinburgh in 1891 (*The Drama: Addresses by Henry Irving* [Boston: Joseph Knight Co., 1892], pp. 82, 186).
17. Bram Stoker, *Personal Reminiscences of Henry Irving* (London: W. Heinemann, 1906), 1:210.
18. Ibid., 2:221-23.
19. "On the Use of Martyrs: Tennyson and Eliot on Thomas Becket," *University of Toronto Quarterly* 33 (1963): 46.
20. "On the Use of Martyrs," p. 59.
21. Charles Tennyson, *Alfred Tennyson* (New York: The Macmillan Co., 1949), p. 465.

Notes to Chapter 4

1. *Browning's Essay on Chatterton* (Cambridge, Mass.: Harvard University Press, 1948), pp. 32-37. I have used the Centenary Edition of Browning's poetry throughout: *The Complete Works of Robert Browning*, ed. Sir Frederic George Kenyon, ten vols. (London: Smith, Elder, and Co., 1912).
2. *The Letters of Robert Browning and Elizabeth Barrett Barrett, 1845-1846* (New York and London: Harper and Brothers, 1899), 1:45. "And what is 'Luria'?" she wrote Browning in February of 1845, "A poem and not a drama? I mean, a poem not in the dramatic form?" (1:22).
3. *Browning's Characters: A Study in Poetic Technique* (New Haven: Yale University Press, 1961).
4. *New Letters of Robert Browning*, ed. William Clyde DeVane and Kenneth Leslie Knickerbocker (New Haven: Yale University Press, 1950), p. 20.
5. *The Diaries of William Charles Macready, 1835-1851*, ed. William Toynbee (New York: G. P. Putnam's Sons, 1912), 2:72. Three weeks later he said of Browning, "I fear he is for ever gone" (2:76). For an account of the Browning-Macready relationship, see Joseph W. Reed, Jr., "Browning and Macready: The Final Quarrel," *PMLA* 75 (1960): 597-603.
6. *Letters of Robert Browning*, ed. Thurman L. Hood (New Haven: Yale University Press, 1933), p. 5.
7. *Diaries of Macready*, 1:362.
8. *Camille and Other Plays*, ed. Stephen S. Stanton (New York: Hill and Wang, 1957), p. xxvi. Stanton's introduction is an excellent analysis of the history and form of the *pièce bien faite*.
9. Ibid., pp. xii-xiii. My discussion of *A Blot* parallels the "well-made" formula as described by Stanton in detail on pages xiv-xv.
10. Ibid., p. xv.
11. "Browning and Experimental Drama," p. 986. McCormick's article is among the best recent essays on Browning's dramas. See also Honan, *Browning's Characters*, especially pp. 41-103, and Roma A. King, Jr., *The Focusing Artifice: The Poetry of Robert Browning* (Athens: Ohio University Press, 1968), pp. 30-63. Robert Langbaum's seminal study *The Poetry of Experience* is of central significance to any study of Browning's use of form.

12. *Letters, 1845-1846*, 1:28.

13. *Elizabeth Barrett to Miss Mitford*, ed. Betty Miller (New Haven: Yale University Press, 1954), p. 179.

14. *The Focusing Artifice*, p. 48. My discussion of *Pippa Passes* owes a considerable debt to King's essay and, to a lesser degree, to Jacob Korg's essay, "A Reading of *Pippa Passes*," *Victorian Poetry* 6 (1968): 5-19; W. David Shaw's *The Dialectical Temper: The Rhetorical Art of Robert Browning* (Ithaca: Cornell University Press, 1968), pp. 45-53; and Honan, *Browning's Characters*, pp. 79-92. Other major studies include the following: D. C. Wilkinson, "The Need for Disbelief: A Comment on *Pippa Passes*," *University of Toronto Quarterly* 29 (1960): 139-51; Margaret Eleanor Glen, "The Meaning and Structure of *Pippa Passes*," *University of Toronto Quarterly* 24 (1955): 410-26; I. M. Ariail, "Is 'Pippa Passes' a Dramatic Failure?" *Studies in Philology* 37 (1940): 120-29; Norton B. Crowell, *The Triple Soul: Browning's Theory of Knowledge* (Albuquerque: University of New Mexico Press, 1963), pp. 161-71.

15. *The Alien Vision of Victorian Poetry*, p. 86.

16. *The Focusing Artifice*, p. 47. In differing with the common dismissal of Pippa as an underdeveloped character, two critics have described her in largely psychological terms: Dale Kramer, "Character and Theme in *Pippa Passes*," *Victorian Poetry* 2 (1964): 241-49; and especially Betty Cobey Senescu, "Another Pippa," *Victorian Newsletter*, no. 33 (1968), pp. 8-12. Although both essays are justified in defending Pippa against traditional critical opinion, Senescu's essay especially exaggerates her prominence as a character.

17. "A Reading of *Pippa Passes*," p. 12.

18. "Browning as Dramatist," *Bulletin of the John Rylands Library* 23 (1939): 66. Charlton praises Browning highly, yet he cannot help but judge him in traditional terms: "But drama is a corporate activity, meant for men in such accidental yet not amorphous groups as gather together in a theatre. . . . drama is social in its outlook: it envisages, not God and man as elements in eternity, but a universe in which God and men are components of a world-order . . ." (p. 34).

19. *Byron as Critic* (1923; reprint ed., New York: Haskell House, 1964), pp. 116-17.

20. McCormick, "Browning and Experimental Drama," pp. 989-90.

21. Hood ed., *Letters*, p. 235.

Notes to Chapter 5

1. Several critics have suggested that modern English drama is a return to primitive dramatic forms. The idea is most fully explored in M. C. Bradbrook's *English Dramatic Form: A History of Its Development* (New York: Barnes and Noble, Inc., 1965). She contends that the medieval form of ritual (the medieval pageantry of Icons and Images, culminating in Marlowe, and the courtly games (which Chaucer used in his dream visions) culminating in Lyly) reappears in much modern drama. But it must be added that whereas medieval drama is based upon ethnic ritual, the "ritual" in modern drama is more often idiosyncratic; the "dream" exists not in "the life of the imagination" (p. 76) but as a psychic reality. Bradbrook says that the "private drama" of character in early dramas "depends upon . . . confidence and ontological security" (p. 23); but in modern drama the act of "ontologi-

cal security" results in the individual's attempt at self-assertion, or, in the extreme case of the Theatre of the Absurd or Theatre of Cruelty, in the inability to articulate at all except in violence and absurdity. Professor Bradbrook represents the common critical attitude toward nineteenth-century drama: she totally ignores it.

2. Martin Lamm, *Modern Drama*, trans. Karin Elliot (Oxford: Basil Blackwood, 1952), p. xiii. The young Friedrich Schlegel wrote in 1795-1796, "Hamlets Stimmung und Richtung nehmlich ist ein Resultat seiner äussern Lage; Fausts ähnliche Richtung ist ursprünglicher Charakter" (*Prosaische Jugendschriften*, 1:114).

3. Bradbrook, *English Dramatic Form*, p. 108.

4. *The Theatre of Revolt*, p. 17. Patricia Ball calls *Cain* and *Prometheus Unbound* "dramas of the moment in the English imagination when self-consciousness becomes a creative force, when the Magus Zoroaster meets his own image walking in the garden. The Lyric Poet now finds he needs a stage—though not necessarily a theatre—peopled with spirits and demons, located anywhere in the cosmos, and dominated by one central consciousness, his own causing all else to be, and throwing around it the unifying illumination which is the awareness of its complex self" (*The Central Self*, p. 55).

5. Robert Langbaum, "Aristotle and Modern Literature," *Journal of Aesthetics and Art Criticism* 15 (1956): 84.

6. *Notes from Underground, Poor People, The Friend of the Family*, trans. Constance Garnett with a general introduction by Ernest J. Simmons (New York: Dell Publishing Co., Inc., 1960), p. 46.

7. The phrase belongs to Bradbrook, *English Dramatic Form*, p. 101.

8. *The Disappearance of God*, p. 12.

9. Ibid., p. 9.

10. *The Playwright as Thinker: A Study of Drama in Modern Times* (1946; reprint ed., Cleveland and New York: The World Publishing Co., 1963), p. 130. In the first three chapters Bentley divides modern drama into two traditions which developed in the nineteenth century: "Tragedy in Modern Dress" (the "realists") and "Tragedy in Fancy Dress" (their "opponents"). His discussion is illuminating, if schematic.

11. *A History of English Drama, 1660-1900*, 4:63.

12. Preface to *Poems*, 1853. Beddoes wrote, "Say what you will—I am convinced the man who is to awaken the drama must be a bold trampling fellow—no creeper into worm-holes—no reviser even—however good. . . . With the greatest reverence for all the antiquities of drama, I still think that we had better beget than revive—attempt to give the literature of this age an idiosyncrasy and spirit of its own, and only raise a ghost to gaze on, not to live with—just now drama is a haunted ruin" (*The Works of Thomas Lovell Beddoes*, ed. H. W. Donner [London: Oxford University Press, 1935], p. 595).

SELECTED BIBLIOGRAPHY

I. HISTORIES OF THE DRAMA

Bernbaum, Ernest. *The Drama of Sensibility: A Sketch of the History of English Sentimental and Domestic Tragedy 1696-1780.* 1915. Reprint. Gloucester, Mass.: Peter Smith, 1958.

Cunliffe, John W. *Modern English Playwrights: A Short History of the English Drama from 1825.* New York and London: Harper and Brothers, Inc., 1927.

Evans, Bertrand. *Gothic Drama from Walpole to Shelley.* Berkeley and Los Angeles: University of California Press, 1947.

Filon, Augustin. *The English Stage: Being an Account of the Victorian Drama.* Translated by Frederic Whyte. New York: Dodd, Mead, and Co., 1897.

Fletcher, Robert McClury. *English Romantic Drama, 1793-1843: A Critical History.* New York: Exposition Press, Inc., 1966.

Ganzel, Dewey. "Patent Wrongs and Patent Theatres: Drama and the Law in the Early Nineteenth Century." *PMLA* 76 (1961): 384-96.

Knight, G. Wilson. *The Golden Labyrinth: A Study of British Drama.* New York: W. W. Norton and Co., Inc., 1962.

Nag, U. C. "The English Theatre of the Romantic Revival," *The Nineteenth Century and After* 104 (1928): 384-98.

Nicoll, Allardyce. *A History of English Drama 1660-1900.* 2d ed. Cambridge: At the University Press, 1959. Vol. 4. *Early Nineteenth Century Drama 1800-1850.*

Reynolds, Ernest. *Early Victorian Drama, 1830-1870.* Cambridge, England: W. Heffner & Sons, Ltd., 1936.

Rhodes, R. Crompton. "The Early Nineteenth-Century Drama." *The Library* 16 (June 1935): 91-112; (September 1935): 210-31.

Rowell, George. *The Victorian Theatre: A Survey.* London: Oxford University Press, 1956.

Stratman, Carl J. "English Tragedy: 1819-1823." *Philological Quarterly* 41 (1962): 465-74.

Watson, Ernest Bradlee. *Sheridan to Robertson: A Study of the Nineteenth-Century English Stage. Cambridge, Mass.: Harvard University Press, 1926.

II. GENERAL HISTORIES AND NINETEENTH-CENTURY SOURCE MATERIAL

Arnold, Matthew. *The Works of Matthew Arnold.* Edition de Luxe. 15 vols. London: Macmillan & Co., 1903-04.

――――. "Letters of an Old Playgoer." In *Discussions of the Drama.* Vol. 4. New York: The Dramatic Museum of Columbia University, 1919.

Bailey, J. O. *British Plays of the Nineteenth Century: An Anthology to Illustrate the Evolution of the Drama.* New York: The Odyssey Press, Inc., 1966.

Barrett, Elizabeth. *Elizabeth Barrett to Miss Mitford.* Edited by Betty Miller. New Haven: Yale University Press, 1954.

Baugh, Albert C., ed. *A Literary History of England.* New York: Appleton-Century-Crofts, Inc., 1948.

Beddoes, Thomas Lovell. *The Works of Thomas Lovell Beddoes.* Edited by H. W. Donner. London: Oxford University Press, 1935.

Brandes, George. *Main Currents in Nineteenth Century Literature.* New York: Boni and Liveright, Inc., 1924. Vol. 4. *Naturalism in England.*

Bulwer and Macready: A Chronicle of the Early Victorian Theatre. Edited by Charles H. Shattuck. Urbana: University of Illinois Press, 1958.

Clark, Barrett H. *European Theories of the Drama.* Cincinnati: Stewart and Kidd Co., 1918.

Coleridge, Samuel Taylor. *Coleridge's Lectures and Notes on Shakespeare and Other English Poets.* Edited by T. Ashe. London: George Bell and Sons, 1900.

――――. *Coleridge's Miscellaneous Criticism.* Edited by Thomas Middleton Raysor. London: Constable and Co., 1936.

――――. *Coleridge's Shakespearean Criticism.* Edited by Thomas Middleton Raysor. Cambridge, Mass.: Harvard University Press, 1930.

――――. *Collected Letters of Samuel Taylor Coleridge.* Edited by E. L. Griggs. 4 vols. Oxford: Clarendon Press, 1956-1959.

――――. *The Notebooks of Samuel Taylor Coleridge.* Edited by Kathleen Coburn. 2 double vols. New York: Pantheon; London: Routledge and Kegan Paul, 1957-1962.

Elton, Oliver. *A Survey of English Literature 1780-1880.* New York: The Macmillan Co., 1920.

Grauel, George E. "The Decline of Tragedy in the Early Nineteenth Century." Ph.D. dissertation, St. Louis University, 1938.

Hazlitt, William. *Hazlitt on Theatre.* Edited by William Archer and Robert Lowe. 1895. Reprint. New York: Hill and Wang, 1957.

Hunt, Leigh. *Leigh Hunt's Dramatic Criticism 1808-1831.* Edited by Lawrence Huston Houtchens and Carolyn Washburn Houtchens. New York: Columbia University Press, 1949.

Irving, Sir Henry. *The Drama: Addresses by Henry Irving.* Boston: Joseph Knight Co., 1892.

James, Henry. *The Complete Plays of Henry James.* Edited by Leon Edel. Philadelphia: J. P. Lippincott Co., 1949.

———. *Views and Reviews by Henry James.* Edited by LeRoy Phillips. Boston: The Ball Publishing Co., 1908.

Jeffrey, Sir Francis. *Jeffrey's Literary Criticism.* Edited by D. Nichol Smith. London: Humphrey Milford, 1928.

Keats, John. *The Letters of John Keats.* Edited by Maurice Buxton Forman. London: Oxford University Press, 1931.

Landor, Walter Savage. *Complete Works of Walter Savage Landor.* Vols. 1-12 edited by T. E. Welby. Vols. 13-16 edited by Stephen Wheeler. London: Chapman and Hall, 1927-1936.

Life of Percy Bysshe Shelley as Comprised in The Life of Shelley by Thomas Jefferson Hogg. The Recollections of Shelley and Byron by Edward John Trelawny. Memoirs of Shelley by Thomas Love Peacock. Edited by Humbert Wolfe. 2 vols. New York: E. P. Dutton and Co., Inc., 1933.

Macready, William Charles. *The Diaries of William Charles Macready, 1833-1851.* Edited by William Toynbee. 2 vols. New York: G. P. Putnam's Sons, 1912.

Nietzsche, Friedrich. *The Birth of Tragedy and The Genealogy of Morals.* Translated by Francis Golffing. Garden City, N. Y.: Doubleday and Co., Inc., 1956.

Saintsbury, George. *A History of Nineteenth Century Literature (1780-1895).* 1896. Reprint. New York: The Macmillan Co., 1910.

Schlegel, August Wilhelm. *A Course of Lectures on Dramatic Art and Literature.* Translated by John Black. 2 vols. 2d ed. London: J. Templeman; J. R. Smith, 1840.

Schlegel, Friedrich. *Friedrich Schlegel 1794-1802. Seine Prosaischen Jugendschriften.* Edited by J. Minor. Vienna: Verlagsbuchhandlung Carl Konegen, 1906.

Shakespeare, William. *Shakespeare: The Complete Works.* Edited by G. B. Harrison. New York: Harcourt, Brace & World, Inc., 1952.

Shelley, Mary. *The Letters of Mary W. Shelley.* Edited by Frederick L. Jones. 2 vols. Norman: University of Oklahoma Press, 1946.

———. *Mary Shelley's Journals.* Edited by Frederick L. Jones. Norman: University of Oklahoma Press, 1947.

Stanton, Stephen S., ed. *Camille and Other Plays.* New York: Hill and Wang, 1957.

Stoker, Bram. *Personal Reminiscences of Henry Irving.* 2 vols. London: W. Heinemann, 1906.

Varma, Devendra P. *The Gothic Flame: Being a History of the Gothic Novel in England: Its Origins, Efflorescence, Disintegration, and Residuary Influences.* London: Arthur Barker, 1957.

III. GENERAL CRITICISM

Abrams, M. H. *The Mirror and the Lamp: The Romantic Theory and the Critical Tradition.* New York: Oxford University Press, 1953.

Bibliography

————, ed. *English Romantic Poets: Modern Essays in Criticism.* New York: Oxford University Press, 1960.

Albrecht, W. P. "Hazlitt's Preference for Tragedy." *PMLA* 71 (1956): 1042-51.

Auerbach, Erich. *Mimesis: The Representation of Reality in Western Literature.* Translated by William Trask. Garden City, N. Y.: Doubleday and Co., Inc., 1953; first published in Berne, Switzerland, 1946.

Babbit, Irving. *Rousseau and Romanticism.* 5th ed. New York: Meridian Books, 1960.

Ball, Patricia. *The Central Self: A Study in Romantic and Victorian Imagination.* London: Athlone Press, 1968.

Barzun, Jacques. *Romanticism and the Modern Ego.* Boston: Little, Brown and Co., 1945.

Bate, Walter Jackson. *From Classic to Romantic: Premises of Taste in Eighteenth Century England.* 1946. Reprint. New York: Harper & Row, Publishers, 1961.

Bentley, Eric. *The Playwright as Thinker: A Study of Drama in Modern Times.* 1946. Reprint. New York: The World Publishing Co., 1963.

Bloom, Harold. *The Visionary Company: A Reading of English Romantic Poetry.* Garden City, N. Y.: Doubleday and Co., 1961.

Bostetter, Edward E. *The Romantic Ventriloquists: Wordsworth, Coleridge, Keats, Shelley, Byron.* Seattle: University of Washington Press, 1963.

Bradbrook, M. C. *English Dramatic Form: A History of Its Development.* New York: Barnes and Noble, Inc., 1965.

Brooke, Stopford A. *Naturalism in English Poetry.* New York: E. P. Dutton and Co., 1920.

Brustein, Robert Sanford. *The Theatre of Revolt: An Approach to the Modern Drama.* Boston: Little, Brown and Co., 1964.

Bush, Douglas. *Mythology and the Romantic Tradition in English Literature.* 1937. Reprint. New York: W. W. Norton and Co., 1963.

Clive, Geoffrey. *The Romantic Enlightenment.* New York: Meridian Books, 1960.

Cunliffe, John W. *Leaders of the Victorian Revolution.* New York: W. Appleton-Century, Co., 1934.

Dickinson, Thomas H. *The Contemporary Drama of England.* Boston: Little, Brown and Co., 1917.

Donohue, Joseph W., Jr. "Hazlitt's Sense of the Dramatic: Actor as Tragic Character." *Studies in English Literature* 5 (1965): 705-21.

Ehrstine, John W. "The Drama and Romantic Theory: The Cloudy Symbols of High Romance." *Research Studies* 34 (1966): 85-106.

Eliot, T. S. *Selected Essays.* New York: Harcourt, Brace and Co., 1950.

Fairchild, Hoxie Neale. *The Romantic Quest.* Philadelphia: Albert Saifer, 1931.

Fergusson, Francis. *The Idea of a Theatre: A Study of Ten Plays in Changing Perspective.* Princeton: Princeton University Press, 1949.

Fricker, Robert. "Shakespeare und das Englische Romantische Drama." *Shakespeare Jahrbuch* 95 (1959): 63-81.

163

Frye, Northrop. *Anatomy of Criticism: Four Essays*. Princeton: Princeton University Press, 1957.

———. *A Study of English Romanticism*. New York: Random House, Inc., 1968.

Hardy, Barbara. " 'I Have a Smack of Hamlet': Coleridge and Shakespeare's Characters." *Essays in Criticism* 8 (1958): 238-55.

Hayden, Donald. "Toward an Understanding of Wordsworth's *The Borderers*." *Modern Language Notes* 66 (1951): 1-6.

Heller, Erich. *The Disinherited Mind*. New York: Meridian Books, 1965.

Herford, C. H. *The Age of Wordsworth*. London: George Bell and Sons, 1911.

Johnson, E. D. H. *The Alien Vision of Victorian Poetry: Sources of the Poetic Imagination in Tennyson, Browning, and Arnold*. Princeton: Princeton University Press, 1952.

Kermode, Frank. *Romantic Image*. London: Routledge and Kegan Paul, 1957.

Kitto, H. D. F. *Greek Tragedy: A Literary Study*. 1939. Reprint. Garden City, N. Y.: Doubleday and Co., 1954.

Knight, G. Wilson. *The Burning Oracle: Studies in the Poetry of Action*. London and New York: Oxford University Press, 1939.

Krutch, Joseph Wood. *The Modern Temper: A Study and a Confession*. New York: Harcourt, Brace and Co., 1929.

Lamm, Martin. *Modern Drama*. Translated by Karin Elliot. Oxford: Basil Blackwell, 1952.

Langbaum, Robert. "Aristotle and Modern Literature." *The Journal of Aesthetics and Art Criticism* 15 (1956): 74-84.

———. *The Poetry of Experience: The Dramatic Monologue in Modern Literary Tradition*. New York: Random House, Inc., 1957.

Lord, Catherine. "Tragedy Without Characters: Poetics VI. 1450ª24." *Journal of Aesthetics and Art Criticism* 28 (1969): 55-62.

Miller, J. Hillis. *The Disappearance of God: Five Nineteenth-Century Writers*. Cambridge, Mass.: Harvard University Press, 1963.

Miyoshi, Masao. *The Divided Self: A Perspective on the Literature of the Victorians*. New York: New York University Press, 1969.

Peacock, Ronald. *The Art of Drama*. London: Routledge and Kegan Paul, 1957.

———. *The Poet in the Theatre*. New York: Harcourt, Brace and Co., 1946.

Peckham, Morse. *Beyond the Tragic Vision: The Quest for Identity in the Nineteenth Century*. New York: George Braziller, Inc., 1962.

Perkins, David. *The Quest for Permanence: The Symbolism of Wordsworth, Shelley, and Keats*. Cambridge, Mass.: Harvard University Press, 1959.

Praz, Mario. *The Romantic Agony*. Translated by Angus Davidson. 2d ed. 1951. Reprint. New York: The World Publishing Co., 1963; first published in 1933.

Prior, Moody E. *The Language of Tragedy*. 1947. Reprint. Bloomington: Indiana University Press, 1966.

Railo, Eino. *The Haunted Castle: A Study of the Elements of English Romanticism.* New York: E. P. Dutton and Co., 1927.

Reinterpretation of Victorian Literature. Edited by Joseph E. Baker. Princeton: Princeton University Press, 1950.

Rodway, Allan. *The Romantic Conflict.* London: Chatto and Windus, 1963.

Ruotolo, Lucio R. "Existentialism and the English Romantic Movement." Ph.D. dissertation, Columbia University, 1960.

Slote, Bernice. *Keats and the Dramatic Principle.* Lincoln: University of Nebraska Press, 1958.

Steiner, George. *The Death of Tragedy.* London: Faber and Faber, 1961.

Viebrock, Helmut. "Shakespeare und die Englische Romantik." *Shakespeare Jahrbuch* 97 (1961): 34-62.

Wasserman, Earl R. *The Subtler Language: Critical Readings of Neoclassic and Romantic Poems.* Baltimore: The Johns Hopkins Press, 1959.

Wellek, René, and Warren, Austin. *Theory of Literature.* 2d ed. New York: Harcourt, Brace and Co., 1956.

Wellwarth, George. *The Theater of Protest and Paradox: Developments in the Avant-Garde Drama.* New York: New York University Press, 1964.

IV. INDIVIDUAL AUTHORS

A. Robert Browning

Ariail, I. M. "Is 'Pippa Passes' a Dramatic Failure?" *Studies in Philology* 37 (1940): 120-29.

Barnett, Howard Albert. "Robert Browning and the Drama: Browning's Plays Viewed in the Context of the Victorian Theatre: 1830-1850." Ph.D. dissertation, Indiana University, 1959.

Browning, Robert. *Browning's Essay on Chatterton.* Edited by Donald Smalley. Cambridge, Mass.: Harvard University Press, 1948.

————. *The Complete Works of Robert Browning.* Edited by Sir F. G. Kenyon. 10 vols. London: Smith, Elder & Co., 1912.

————. *Letters of Robert Browning.* Edited by Thurman L. Hood. New Haven: Yale University Press, 1933.

————. *Letters of Robert Browning and Elizabeth Barrett Barrett, 1845-1846.* 2 vols. New York and London: Harper and Brothers, Publishers, 1899.

————. *New Letters of Robert Browning.* Edited by William Clyde DeVane and Kenneth Leslie Knickerbocker. New Haven: Yale University Press, 1950.

————. *Robert Browning and Julia Wedgwood: A Broken Friendship as Revealed by Their Letters.* Edited by Richard Curle. New York: Frederick A. Stokes Co., 1937.

Charlton, H. B. "Browning as Dramatist." *Bulletin of the John Rylands Library* 23 (1939): 33-67.

Clarke, George Herbert. "Browning's *A Blot in the 'Scutcheon*: A Defense." *Sewanee Review* 28 (1920): 213-27.

Collins, Thomas J. *Robert Browning's Moral-Aesthetic Theory, 1833-1855.* Lincoln: University of Nebraska Press, 1967.

Crowell, Norton B. *The Triple Soul: Browning's Theory of Knowledge.* Albuquerque: University of New Mexico Press, 1963.

Curry, S. S. *Browning and the Dramatic Monologue.* Boston: Expression Co., 1908.

DeVane, William Clyde. *A Browning Handbook.* 2d ed. New York: Appleton-Century-Crofts, 1955.

Dubois, Arthur E. "Robert Browning, Dramatist." *Studies in Philology* 33 (1936): 626-55.

Faverty, Frederic E. "The Source of the Jules-Phene Episode in *Pippa Passes.*" *Studies in Philology* 38 (1941): 97-105.

Glen, Margaret Eleanor. "The Meaning and Structure of *Pippa Passes.*" *University of Toronto Quarterly* 24 (1955): 410-26.

Hill, Archibald A. "Pippa's Song: Two Attempts at Structural Criticism." *University of Texas Studies in English* 35 (1956): 51-56.

Honan, Park. *Browning's Characters: A Study in Poetic Technique.* New Haven: Yale University Press, 1961.

Johnson, Charles E., Jr. "The Dramatic Career of Robert Browning: A Survey and Analysis." Ph.D. dissertation, Duke University, 1958.

Jones, Henry. "Browning as a Dramatic Poet." In *The Boston Browning Society Papers from 1886-1897.* New York, 1900, pp. 203-20.

King, Roma A., Jr. *The Focusing Artifice: The Poetry of Robert Browning.* Athens: Ohio University Press, 1968.

Korg, Jacob. "A Reading of *Pippa Passes.*" *Victorian Poetry* 6 (1968): 5-19.

Kramer, Dale. "Character and Theme in *Pippa Passes.*" *Victorian Poetry* 2 (1964): 241-49.

Langbaum, Robert. "Browning and the Question of Myth." *PMLA* 81 (1969): 575-84.

Litzinger, Boyd, and Knickerbocker, K. L. *The Browning Critics.* Lexington: University of Kentucky Press, 1965.

Lounsbury, Thomas R. *The Early Literary Career of Robert Browning.* New York: Charles Scribner's Sons, 1911.

Lubbock, Percy. "Robert Browning." *The Quarterly Review* 217 (1912): 437-57.

McCormick, James Patton. "Robert Browning and the Experimental Drama." *PMLA* 68 (1953): 982-91.

Orr, Mrs. Sutherland. *A Handbook to the Works of Robert Browning.* London: George Bell and Sons, 1910.

Otten, Terry. "What Browning Never Learned from Bulwer-Lytton." *Research Studies* 37 (1969): 338-42.

Phelps, William Lyon. "Browning as Dramatist." *Yale Review* 1 (1912): 551-67.

Pottle, Frederick A. *Shelley and Browning: A Myth and Some Facts.* Chicago: Pembroke Press, 1923.

Purcell, J. M. "The Dramatic Failure of *Pippa Passes.*" *Studies in Philology* 36 (1939): 77-87.

Raymond, William O. *The Infinite Moment and Other Essays in Robert Browning*. Toronto: University of Toronto Press, 1959.

Reed, Joseph W., Jr. "Browning and Macready: The Final Quarrel." *PMLA* 75 (1960): 597-603.

Russell, Frances Theresa. "Browning's Account with Tragedy." *Sewanee Review* 31 (1923): 87-99.

Senescu, Betty Cobey. "Another Pippa." *Victorian Newsletter* 33 (1968): 8-12.

Shaw, W. David. *The Dialectical Temper: The Rhetorical Art of Robert Browning*. Ithaca: Cornell University Press, 1968.

Ward, Maisie. *Robert Browning and His World: The Private Face, 1812-1861*. New York: Holt, Rinehart and Winston, 1967.

Wilkinson, D. C. "The Need for Disbelief: A Comment on *Pippa Passes*." *University of Toronto Quarterly* 29 (1960): 139-51.

B.   George Gordon, Lord Byron

Butler, E. M. *Byron and Goethe: Analysis of a Passion*. London: Bowes and Bowes, 1956.

Byron, George Gordon, Lord. *Byron: A Self-Portrait: Letters and Diaries 1798-1824*. Edited by Peter Quennell. 2 vols. New York: Charles Scribner's Sons, 1950.

————. *His Very Self and Voice: Collected Conversations of Lord Byron*. Edited by Ernest J. Lovell, Jr. New York: The Macmillan Co., 1954.

————. *Lord Byron's Correspondence, Chiefly with Lady Melbourne, Mr. Hobhouse, the Hon. Douglas Kinnaird, and P. B. Shelley*. Edited by John Murray. 2 vols. New York: Charles Scribner's Sons, 1922.

————. *The Works of Lord Byron. Poetry*. Edited by Ernest Hartley Coleridge. 7 vols. London: J. Murray Co.; New York: Charles Scribner's Sons, 1898-1905.

————. *The Works of Lord Byron. Letters and Journals*. Edited by Rowland E. Prothero. 6 vols. London: J. Murray Co.; New York: Charles Scribner's Sons, 1898-1905.

Calvert, William. *Byron: Romantic Paradox*. Chapel Hill: University of North Carolina Press, 1935.

Chew, Samuel C. *The Dramas of Lord Byron: A Critical Study*. 1915. Reprint. New York: Russell and Russell, 1964.

Cooke, Michael G. "The Limits of Skepticism: The Byronic Affirmation." *Keats-Shelley Journal* 17 (1968): 97-111.

Drinkwater, John. *The Pilgrim of Eternity: Byron—A Conflict*. New York: George H. Doran Co., 1925.

Elledge, W. Paul. *Byron and the Dynamics of Metaphor*. Nashville: Vanderbilt University Press, 1968.

Erdman, David V. "Byron's Stage Fright: The History of his Ambition and Fear of Writing for the Stage." *ELH* 6 (1939): 219-43.

Escarpit, Robert. *Lord Byron: un tempérament littéraire*. Paris: Le Cercle Du Livre, 1957.

Evans, Bertrand. "Manfred's Remorse and Dramatic Tradition." *PMLA* 62 (1947): 752-73.

Gleckner, Robert F. *Byron and the Ruins of Paradise*. Baltimore: The Johns Hopkins Press, 1967.

Goode, Clement Tyson. *Byron as Critic*. 1923. Reprint. New York: Haskell House, 1964.

Hassler, Donald. "*Marino Faliero*, The Byronic Hero, and *Don Juan*." *Keats-Shelley Journal* 14 (1965): 55-64.

Joseph, M. K. *Byron: The Poet*. London: Gollancz, 1964.

Knight, G. Wilson. "Byron and *Hamlet*." *Bulletin of the John Rylands Library* 45 (1962): 115-47.

————. *Byron's Dramatic Prose*. Nottingham: University of Nottingham, 1953.

————. "Shakespeare and Byron's Plays." *Shakespeare Jahrbuch* 95 (1959): 82-97.

Marchand, Leslie A. *Byron: A Biography*. 3 vols. New York: Alfred A. Knopf, Inc., 1957.

Marshall, William H. *The Structure of Byron's Major Poems*. Philadelphia: University of Pennsylvania Press, 1962.

Maurois, André. *Byron*. Translated by Hamish Miles. New York: D. Appleton and Co., 1930.

Mayne, Ethel Colburn. *Byron*. New York: Charles Scribner's Sons, 1913.

Michaels, Leonard. "Byron's *Cain*." *PMLA* 84 (1969): 71-78.

Motter, T. H. Vail. "Byron's *Werner* Re-estimated: A Neglected Chapter in Nineteenth-Century Stage History." In *The Parrott Presentation Volume*, edited by Hardin Craig. Princeton: Princeton University Press, 1935.

Rutherford, Andrew. *Byron: A Critical Study*. Stanford: Stanford University Press, 1961.

Steffan, Truman Guy. *Lord Byron's Cain: Twelve Essays and a Text with Variants and Annotations*. Austin: University of Texas Press, 1968.

Thorslev, Peter L., Jr. *The Byronic Hero: Types and Prototypes*. Minneapolis: University of Minnesota Press, 1962.

C. Percy Bysshe Shelley

Adams, Charles L. "The Structure of *The Cenci*." *Drama Survey* 4 (1965): 139-48.

Baker, Carlos. *Shelley's Major Poetry: The Fabric of a Vision*. 1948. Reprint. New York: Russell and Russell, Pubs., 1961.

Bald, Marjory A. "Shelley's Mental Progress." In *Essays and Studies by Members of the English Association*, edited by Caroline F. E. Spurgeon. Vol. 13. Oxford, 1928.

Barnard, Ellsworth. *Shelley's Religion*. Minneapolis: University of Minnesota Press, 1937.

Barrell, Joseph. *Shelley and the Thought of his Time*. New Haven: Yale University Press, 1947.

Bates, E. S. *A Study of Shelley's Drama The Cenci*. New York: Columbia University Press, 1908.

Blunden, Edmund. *Shelley: A Life Story*. 1946. Reprint. New York: Viking Press, Inc., 1965.

Butter, Peter. *Shelley's Idols of the Cave.* Edinburgh: At the University Press, 1954.

Cameron, Kenneth N., and Frenz, Horst. "The Stage History of Shelley's *The Cenci.*" *PMLA* 60 (1945): 1080-105.

Campbell, Oliver Ward. *Shelley and the Unromantics.* New York: Charles Scribner's Sons, 1924.

Clark, David L. "Shelley and Shakespeare." *PMLA* 54 (1939): 261-87.

Crompton, Margaret. *Shelley's Dream Women.* London: Cassell, 1967.

Curran, Stuart. *Shelley's Cenci: Scorpions Ringed with Fire.* Princeton: Princeton University Press, 1970.

Donohue, Joseph W., Jr. "Shelley's Beatrice and the Romantic Concept of Tragic Character." *Keats-Shelley Journal* 17 (1968): 53-73.

Dowden, Edward. *The Life of Percy Bysshe Shelley.* 2 vols. London: Kegan Paul, French and Co., 1886.

Duerksen, Roland A. "Shelley and Shaw." *PMLA* 78 (1963): 114-27.

Elledge, W. Paul. "Good, Evil, and the Function of Art: A Note on Shelley." *Tennessee Studies in Literature* 14 (1969): 87-92.

Grabo, Carl. *The Magic Plant: The Growth of Shelley's Thought.* Chapel Hill: University of North Carolina Press, 1936.

Hughes, A. M. D. *The Nascent Mind of Shelley.* Oxford: Clarendon Press, 1947.

Hurt, James R. "*Prometheus Unbound* and Aeschylean Dramaturgy." *Keats-Shelley Journal* 15 (1966): 43-48.

Kessel, Marcel, and States, Bert O., Jr. "*The Cenci* as a Stage Play." *PMLA* 75 (1960): 147-49.

King-Hele, Desmond. *Shelley: The Man and the Poet.* New York: Thomas Yoseloff, Inc., 1960.

Kurtz, Benjamin P. *The Pursuit of Death: A Study of Shelley's Poetry.* London: Oxford University Press, 1933.

Langston, Beach. "Shelley's Use of Shakespeare." *Huntington Library Quarterly* 12 (1949): 163-90.

Marshall, William H. "*Caleb Williams* and *The Cenci.*" *Notes and Queries*, no. 7 (1960), pp. 260-68.

Medwin, Thomas. *The Life of Percy Bysshe Shelley.* London: Oxford University Press, 1913.

Mesterházi, Márton. "Shelley A Cenciek c. drámája és az angol reneszánsz tragédia." *Filologiai Közlöny* 14 (1968): 207-17. [Shelley's *The Cenci* and English renaissance tragedy]

Otten, Terry. "Christabel, Beatrice, and the Encounter with Evil." *Bucknell Review* 17 (1969): 19-31.

Pulos, C. E. *The Deep Truth: A Study of Shelley's Scepticism.* Lincoln: University of Nebraska Press, 1954.

Rees, Joan. "The Preface to *The Cenci.*" *Review of English Studies* 8 (1957): 172-73.

————. "Shelley's Orsino: Evil in *The Cenci.*" *Keats-Shelley Memorial Bulletin* 12 (1961): 3-8.

Reiter, Seymour. *A Study of Shelley's Poetry.* Albuquerque: University of New Mexico Press, 1967.

Ridenour, George M., ed. *Shelley: A Collection of Critical Essays.* Englewood Cliffs, N. J.: Prentice-Hall, 1965.

Rieger, James. *The Mutiny Within: The Heresies of Percy Bysshe Shelley.* New York: George Braziller, Inc., 1967.

Rogers, Neville. *Shelley at Work: A Critical Inquiry.* Oxford: Clarendon Press, 1956.

Schulze, Earl J. *Shelley's Theory of Poetry: A Reappraisal.* The Hague: Mouton, 1966.

Shelley, Percy Bysshe. *The Complete Works of Percy Bysshe Shelley.* Edited by Thomas Hutchinson. London: Oxford University Press, 1905; New York: Oxford University Press, 1951.

————. *The Complete Works of Percy Bysshe Shelley.* Edited by Roger Ingpen and Walter E. Peck. 10 vols. New York: Charles Scribner's Sons, 1926-1930.

————. *The Letters of Percy Bysshe Shelley.* Edited by R. Brimsley Johnson. New York: Dodd, Mead and Co., 1929.

————. *Shelley's Prose: The Trumpet of a Prophecy.* Edited by David Lee Clark. Albuquerque: University of New Mexico Press, 1954.

Solve, Melvin T. *Shelley: His Theory of Poetry.* 1927. Reprint. New York: Russell and Russell, 1964.

States, Bert O., Jr. "Addendum: The Stage History of Shelley's *The Cenci.*" *PMLA* 72 (1957): 633-44.

Steffan, Truman Guy. "Seven Accounts of *The Cenci* and Shelley's Drama." *Studies in English Literature* 9 (1969): 601-18.

Stovall, Floyd. *Desire and Restraint in Shelley.* Durham: Duke University Press, 1931.

Symonds, John Addington. *Shelley.* New York: The Macmillan Co., 1902.

Watson, Melvin R. "Shelley and Tragedy: The Case of Beatrice Cenci." *Keats-Shelley Journal* 7 (1958): 13-21.

Watson, Sara R. "Shelley and Shakespeare: An Addendum; a Comparison of *Othello* and *The Cenci.*" *PMLA* 55 (1940): 611-14.

White, Newman Ivey. *Shelley.* 2 vols. New York: Alfred A. Knopf, Inc., 1940.

————. *The Unextinguished Hearth: Shelley and his Contemporary Critics.* Durham: Duke University Press, 1938.

Whitman, Robert F. "Beatrice's 'Pernicious Mistake' in *The Cenci.*" *PMLA* 74 (1959): 249-53.

Wilson, Milton Thomas. *Shelley's Later Poetry: A Study of his Prophetic Imagination.* New York: Columbia University Press, 1959.

Winstanley, L. "Platonism in Shelley." In *Essays and Studies by Members of the English Association,* edited by C. H. Herford. Vol. 4. Oxford, 1913.

Woodings, R. B. " 'A Devil of a Nut to Crack': Shelley's *Charles the First.*" *Studia Neophilologica* 40 (1968): 216-37.

Wright, Walter F. "Shelley's Failure in *Charles I.*" *ELH* 8 (1941): 41-46.

D. Alfred Lord Tennyson

Basler, Roy P. "Tennyson the Psychologist." *South Atlantic Quarterly* 43 (1944): 142-59.

Bibliography

Baum, Paull F. *Tennyson Sixty Years After*. Chapel Hill: University of North Carolina Press, 1948.

Benson, Arthur Christopher. *Alfred Tennyson*. New York: E. P. Dutton and Co., 1907.

Brooke, Stopford A. *Tennyson: His Art and Relation to Modern Life*. New York: G. P. Putnam's Sons, 1903.

Buckley, Jerome Hamilton. *Tennyson: The Growth of a Poet*. Cambridge, Mass.: Harvard University Press, 1960.

Cary, Elisabeth L. *Tennyson: His Homes, His Friends and His Works*. New York: G. P. Putnam's Sons, 1898.

Fausset, Hugh I'Anson. *Tennyson: A Modern Portrait*. New York: D. Appleton and Co., 1923.

Harrison, Thomas P. "Tennyson's *Maud* and Shakespeare." *Shakespeare Association Bulletin* 17 (1942): 80-85.

Japikse, C. G. H. *The Dramas of Alfred Lord Tennyson*. New York: The Macmillan Co., 1926.

Johnson, E. D. H. "The Lily and the Rose: Symbolic Meaning in Tennyson's 'Maud.'" *PMLA* 64 (1949): 1222-27.

Killham, John, ed. *Critical Essays on the Poetry of Tennyson*. London: Routledge and Kegan Paul, 1960.

Lyall, Sir Alfred. *Tennyson*. New York: The Macmillan Co., 1910.

Pitt, Valerie. *Tennyson Laureate*. Toronto: University of Toronto Press, 1963.

Radar, Ralph Wilson. *Tennyson's Maud: The Biographical Genesis*. Berkeley and Los Angeles: University of California Press, 1964.

Rehak, Louise Rouse. "On the Use of Martyrs: Tennyson and Eliot on Thomas Becket." *University of Toronto Quarterly* 33 (1963): 43-60.

Ryals, Clyde de L. "Tennyson's 'Maud.'" *Connotation* 1 (1962): 12-32.

Smith, Elton Edward. *The Two Voices: A Tennyson Study*. Lincoln: University of Nebraska Press, 1964.

Steane, J. B. *Tennyson*. London: Evans Brothers, 1966.

Stokes, Edward. "The Metrics of *Maud*." *Victorian Poetry* 2 (1964): 97-110.

Tennyson, Alfred Lord. *The Works of Alfred Lord Tennyson*. Edited by Hallam Lord Tennyson. 6 vols. London: Macmillan & Co., 1908.

Tennyson, Charles. *Alfred Tennyson*. New York: The Macmillan Co., 1949.

Tennyson, Hallam Lord. *Alfred Lord Tennyson: A Memoir by his Son*. 2 vols. New York: The Macmillan Co., 1911.

Van Dyke, Henry. *Studies in Tennyson*. New York: Charles Scribner's Sons, 1921.

Wolfe, Humbert. *Tennyson*. London: Faber and Faber, 1930.

INDEX

Abrams, M. H., 153; *The Mirror and the Lamp*, 150

Action, as opposed to plot, 12, 22

Adams, Charles L., 152

Alfieri, Vittorio, 15, 41

Anouilh, Jean, 149

Ariail, J. M., 158

Aristophanes, 141

Aristotle (Aristotelian), 5, 7, 9, 10, 13, 14, 18, 19, 33, 94, 141, 146, 150, 151

Arnold, Matthew, *Empedocles on Etna*, 78; "French Play in London," 8; Preface to *Poems* (1853), 4, 149, 159

Auerbach, Erich, *Mimesis* (trans. by Willard Trask), 6-7, 151

Babbitt, Irving, *Rousseau and Romanticism*, 8, 74, 151, 155

Bailey, J. O., *British Plays of the Nineteenth Century*, 151

Baker, Carlos, *Shelley's Major Poetry*, 153

Ball, Patricia, *The Central Self*, 151, 156, 159

Bancroft(s), Squire and Marie, 91, 93, 94

Baring, Rosa, 85

Barrell, Joseph, *Shelley and the Thought of His Time*, 153

Barrett, Elizabeth, 111, 122, 157, 158

Basler, Roy P., 155, 156

Bate, Walter Jackson, *From Classic to Romantic*, 151

Bates, Ernest Sutherland, *A Study of Shelley's Drama The Cenci*, 152

Baum, Paull, *Tennyson Sixty Years After*, 91, 92, 156, 157

Beddoes, Thomas Lovell, 159

Bentley, Eric, *The Playwright as Thinker*, 148, 159

Bernbaum, Ernest, *The Drama of Sensibility*, 151

Blake, William (Blakean), 20, 27

Bloom, Harold, *The Visionary Company*, 61, 154

Blunden, Edmund, *Shelley: A Life Story*, 16, 152

Bostetter, Edward, *The Romantic Ventriloquists*, 61, 154

Boucicault, Dion, 141

Bradbrook, M. C., *English Dramatic Form*, 144, 158-59

Bradley, A. C., *Shakespearean Tragedy*, 6, 150-51

Brooke, Stopford, *Naturalism in English Poetry*, 65, 154

Browning, Robert, 10, 11-12, 78, 107, *108-42*, 144, 146, 147, 148, 157-58; and the stage, 108-12; "Andrea Del Sarto," 108, 131, 140; *Aristophanes' Apology*, 141; *Blot in the 'Scutcheon, A*, 12, 109, *111-21*, 122, 141, 157; "Cleon," 123; *Colombe's Birthday*, 122; "Essay on

Chatterton," 110, 157; "Essay on Shelley," 17, 110-11; *In a Balcony*, 122; *Luria*, 110, 122, 157; *Paracelsus*, 110; *Pippa Passes*, 12, 110, 111, 122-40, 141, 142, 146, 158; *Return of the Druses*, 111; *Sordello*, 110; *Soul's Tragedy, A*, 110, 122; *Strafford*, 92, 112, 123, 141, Preface to *Strafford*, 7, 110
Brustein, Robert, *The Theatre of Revolt*, 74, 145, 155, 159
Büchner, Georg, *Woyzeck*, 89, 144
Buckley, Jerome, *Tennyson*, 156
Byron, George Gordon, Lord, 10, 18, 41-75, 92, 107, 108, 142, 144, 148, 152, 153-55; attitude toward the theater, 41-43; attempts at drama, 43-45; *Cain*, 11, 12, 43, 44, 45-67, 70, 72, 73, 74, 75, 111, 122, 124, 145, 147, 154-55, 159, and *Manfred*, 45-52, 63-64, and *Faust*, 50, 53, 55-56, and *The Cenci*, 50, 51-52, 53, 54-55, 60, 62, 63; *English Bards and Scotch Reviewers*, 42; "Hints from Horace," 42; *Manfred*, 43, 44, 45, 66, 72, 74, 78, 154, and *Cain*, 45-52, 63-64, *Marino Faliero*, 43, 44, 46, 155; *Sardanapalus*, 43, 44; *The Two Foscari*, 43; *Werner*, 11, 46, 67-72, 111, 154, and *Manfred*, 72

Calderón de la Barca, Pedro, 16, 17
Cameron(s), Charles Hay and Julia, 156
Carwardine, Henry Holgate, 151
Cary, Elisabeth L., *Tennyson*, 155
Charlton, H. B., 130, 158
Chaucer, Geoffrey, 158
Chekhov, Anton, 142, 144; *The Cherry Orchard*, 41
Chew, Samuel, *The Dramas of Lord Byron*, 66, 154
Cocteau, Jean, 145
Coleridge, Ernest Hartley, *The Works of Lord Byron* (Poetry), 154
Coleridge, Samuel Taylor, 29, 92;

concept of organic form, 7; *Biographia Literaria*, 4; *Lectures of 1818*, 6, 7; *Remorse*, 42
Corneille, Pierre, 5
Cornwall, Barry, 18
Correggio, Antonio Allegri da, 133, 137
Covent Garden Theatre, 15, 91
Craig, Hardin, *The Parrott Presentation Volume*, 154
Crowell, Norton B., *The Triple Soul*, 158
Cunliffe, John W., *Leaders of the Victorian Revolution*, 156
Curran, Stuart, *Shelley's Cenci*, 152, 153
Cuvier, George Léopold Chrétien Frédéric Dagobert, Baron, 154

DeVane, William Clyde (and Kenneth Leslie Knickerbocker), *New Letters of Robert Browning*, 157
Donner, H. W., *The Works of Thomas Lovell Beddoes*, 159
Donohue, Joseph W., Jr., 152
Dostoyevsky, Fyodor, 159; *Crime and Punishment*, 37; *Notes from the Underground*, 106, 146
Drama of Sensibility, 151
Drinkwater, John, *The Pilgrim of Eternity*, 73, 155
Drury Lane Theatre, 41, 42, 43, 68, 91

Edel, Leon, *The Complete Plays of Henry James*, 153
Ehrstine, John W., 150
Eliot, T. S., *Murder in the Cathedral*, 99, 105; *The Waste Land*, 155
Erdman, David, 72, 73, 154
Escarpit, Robert, *Lord Byron*, 69, 74, 154, 155
Euripides, 141
Existentialism (existential), 38, 65, 146

Faussett, I'Anson, *Tennyson*, 155
Fitzball, Edward, 141

Flaubert, Gustave, **8**
Fletcher, Richard M., *English Romantic Drama*, 150
Fogle, Richard Harter, *The Imagery of Keats and Shelley*, 153
Ford, John, 16
Freud, Sigmund (Freudian), 31, 149
Fricker, Robert, 151
Frye, Northrop, *Anatomy of Criticism*, 50, 154; *A Study of English Romanticism*, 19, 150, 152

Garrick, David, 90
Gifford, William, 44
Gilbert, William S., Sir, 91, 156
Giraudoux, Jean, 149
Glen, Margaret Eleanor, 158
Goethe, Johann Wolfgang von, 145, 150; *Faust*, 4, 37, 47, 50, 53, 55-56, 67, 79-80, 88, 143-44, 154
Goode, Clement Tyson, *Byron as Critic*, 141, 158
Gothic (Gothicism), 9, 20, 21, 22, 23, 28, 32, 43, 44, 45, 46, 47, 48, 70, 71, 141, 145
Grabo, Carl, *The Magic Plant*, 153
Guido (Reni), 15

Harrison, G. B., *Shakespeare: The Complete Works*, 150-51
Harrison, Thomas P., 155
Hassler, Donald, 155
Hazlitt, William, *Characters of Shakespeare's Plays*, 6
Hebbel, Christian Friedrich, 77, 150; *Journals*, 3; Preface to *Maria Magdalena*, 66-67, 144
Heller, Erich, *The Disinherited Mind*, 154
Heywood, **Thomas**, *A Woman Killed With Kindness*, 97
Hobhouse, John Cam, 67
Hogg, Thomas Jefferson, 152
Holland, Lord, 42
Honan, Park, *Browning's Characters*, 111, 157, 158
Hood, Thurman L., *Letters of Robert Browning*, 157, 158

Hughes, A. M. D., *The Nascent Mind of Shelley*, 15-16, 152
Hugo, Victor, 77, 144
Hutchinson, Thomas, *The Complete Works of Percy Bysshe Shelley*, 152

Ibsen, Henrik, 14, 19, 40, 94, 144, 147; *Ghosts*, 147; *Peer Gynt*, 73
Ingpen, Roger (and Walter E. Peck), *The Complete Works of Percy Bysshe Shelley*, 151-52
Irving, Henry, Sir, 77, 78, 93, 94, 95, 99, 101-02, 106, 157

James, Henry, 40, 153
Jeffrey, Francis, Lord, 72-73, 155
Jerrold, Douglas William, 141
Johnson, E. D. H., 155; *The Alien Vision of Victorian Poetry*, 76, 122, 156, 158
Joseph, M. K., *Byron: The Poet*, 44-45, 153, 154
Jung, Carl (Jungian), 149

Kean, Edmund, 41, 43, 73, 94
Kemble, John, 68, 90
Kenyon, Frederic George, Sir, *The Works of Robert Browning*, 157
Kierkegaard, Soren, *Either/Or* (trans. by Walter Lowrie), 156
Killham, John, *Critical Essays on the Poetry of Tennyson*, 156
King, Roma A., Jr., *The Focusing Artifice*, 122, 123, 124, 157, 158
King-Hele, Desmond, *Shelley*, 152
Korg, Jacob, 129-30, 158
Kotzebue, August Friedrich Ferdinand von, 9
Kramer, Dale, 158
Kurtz, Benjamin P., *The Pursuit of Death*, 152

Lamb, Charles, *On the Tragedies of Shakespeare*, 6
Lamm, Martin, *Modern Drama* (trans. by Karin Elliot), 159

Langbaum, Robert, 159; *The Poetry of Experience*, 5, 56, 88, 150, 151, 154, 156, 157
Lee, Harriet, "Kruitzner," 67, 68
Lessing, Gotthold Ephraim, 150
Lewis, C. S., *Rehabilitations and Other Criticisms*, 153
Lillo, George, *The London Merchant*, 143
Ludwig, Otto, 150
Lyceum, 93
Lyly, John, 158
Lytton, Edward Bulwer, First Baron, 113, 141, 142; *Richelieu*, 113; *Money*, 113

Macready, William Charles, 68, 90, 93, 157; and Browning, 108-09, 111, 112, 113, 157
Marlowe, Christopher (Marlovian), 142, 158
Marshall, William, 152; *The Structure of Byron's Major Poetry*, 63, 154
Massey, Gerald, 155
Massinger, Philip, 15
McCormick, James P., 93, 121, 142, 157, 158
Michaels, Leonard, 64, 154
Milbanke, Anna Isabelle (Lady Byron), 42
Middleton, Thomas, *A Game at Chess*, 97
Miller, Arthur, *After the Fall*, 89
Miller, Betty, *Elizabeth Barrett to Miss Mitford*, 158
Miller, J. Hillis, *The Disappearance of God*, 37, 143, 147-48, 150, 153, 159
Milman, Henry Hart, 18
Milton, John, 106; *Paradise Lost*, 47, 66
Moore, Thomas, 154
Miyoshi, Masao, *The Divided Self*, 28, 152
Morgann, Maurice, *Essay on the Dramatic Character of John Falstaff*, 6

Moscow Art Theatre, 142
Motter, T. A. Vail, 154
Murray, John, 43, 44, 64, 67-68, 73, 153; *Lord Byron's Correspondence*, 154

Nag, U. C., 150
New National Theatre (Hamburg), 150
Nicoll, Allardyce, *A History of English Drama*, 148, 150, 159
Nietzsche, Friedrich Wilhelm (Nietzschean), 67, 144, 148

O'Neill, Eliza, 15
O'Neill, Eugene, 149

Pascal, Blaise, *Pensées*, 13, 21
Patmore, Coventry, 90
Peacock, Ronald, *The Art of Drama*, 155, 156
Peacock, Thomas Love, 14-15; *Memoirs of Percy Bysshe Shelley*, 14, 152
Peckham, Morse, *Beyond the Tragic Vision*, 67, 150, 154
Pinero, Arthur, Sir, 40
Pirandello, Luigi, 73
Pitt, Valerie, *Tennyson Laureate*, 156
Planché, James Robinson, 141
Plato, 153
Plot, as opposed to action, 12, 20
Pollock, Frederick, 90
Prince of Wales's Theatre, 93
Prior, Moody, *The Language of Tragedy*, 13-14, 22, 151, 152
Prothero, Rowland, *The Works of Lord Byron*, (Letters and Journals), 153

Racine, Jean Baptiste, 5, 74, 143
Rader, Ralph, *Tennyson's Maud*, 85, 156
Reed, Joseph W., Jr., 157
Rehak, Louise, 105-06, 157
Reiter, Seymour, *A Study of Shelley's Poetry*, 16, 20, 152

Rieger, James, *The Mutiny Within*, 152

Robertson, Thomas William, 40, 91, 93, 156

Rowell, George, *The Victorian Theatre*, 93-94, 150, 157

Ryals, Clyde de L., 155

Sardou, Viktorien, 94; *Les Premières Armes de figaro*, 113

Sartre, Jean Paul, 149

Schlegel, August Wilhelm von, 150; *Lectures on Dramatic Art and Literature* (trans. by John Black), 5, 150

Schlegel, Friedrich von, 150, 151; "Essay on Greek Poesy," 9, 159

Scribe, Augustin Eugène, 113

Sellwood, Emily, 85

Senescu, Betty Cobey, 158

Shakespeare, William (Shakespearean), 6-11, 16, 17, 18, 19, 44, 66, 74, 77, 91, 94, 105, 106, 110, 119, 121, 142, 144, 147, 150-51, 155; romantics attitude toward, 6-8; *Hamlet*, 4, 6, 11, 38, 66, 78, 79-80, 87-88, 89, 147, 150-51, 155, 159; *King Lear*, 6, 105, 144-45, 147; *Macbeth*, 105; *Othello*, 24, 26, 110; *Romeo and Juliet*, 113, 119

Shaw, George Bernard, 94

Shaw, W. David, *The Dialectical Temper*, 158

Shelley, Mary Godwin, 33; *Journal*, 14; Notes on *The Cenci*, 19, 28, 152

Shelley, Percy Bysshe, 10, *13-40*, 41, 91, 105, 108, 110, 144, 148, 151-53; attitude toward *The Cenci*, 14-15, 18; attitude toward the theater, 14-15; on the nature of drama, 16-18; *Cenci, The*, 10-11, 12, 13, 14, 15, 16, *18-40*, 50, 51-52, 53, 54-55, 60-61, 62, 63, 70, 77, 112, 122, 144, 145, 147, 152-53; Preface to *The Cenci*, 18-20, 28, 29, 34, 39; *Defence of Poetry*, 17, 18; *Hellas*,

16-17; *Prometheus Unbound*, 17, 38, 153, 159, and *The Cenci*, 38, 153; *Revolt of Islam, The*, 153; *Treatise on Morals*, 39; *Triumph of Life, The*, 153

Sheridan, Richard Brinsley, 41, 143, 156

Smalley, Donald, *Browning's Essay on Chatterton*, 110, 157

Smith, D. Nichol, *Jeffrey's Literary Criticism*, 155

Sophocles, 15, 16, 74; *Oedipus Rex*, 74

Stanislavsky, Konstantin, 142

Stanton, Stephen S., *Camille and Other Plays*, 113-14, 115, 119, 157

Steffan, Truman Guy, 152; *Lord Byron's Cain*, 154

Steiner, George, *The Death of Tragedy*, 42, 73, 150, 153, 155

Stoker, Bram, *Personal Reminiscences of Henry Irving*, 94-95, 157

Stokes, Edward, 156

Strindberg, August, 14, 40, 73, 144, 147; *A Dream Play*, 89; Forward to *Miss Julie*, 38, 67; *The Ghost Sonata*, 89; *To Damascus II*, 145

Taylor, Tom, 91, 156

Tennyson, Alfred, Lord, 10, 11, 76-107, 108, 144, 148, 155-57; and the stage, 76-77, 90-95, 196-07; *Becket*, 11, 77, 92, *94-106*, 157, and *Murder in the Cathedral*, 99, 105-06; *Cup, The*, 93; *Devil and the Lady, The*, 90; *Enoch Arden*, 94; *Falcon, The*, 93; *Foresters, The*, 93; *Harold*, 92; *Idylls of the King*, 77, 78, 79, 95, 105; *In Memoriam*, 77, 78, 79, 80; *Maud*, 11, 12, *77-90*, 95, 105, 106-07, 122, 132, 136, 147, 155-56; *Promise of May, The*, 93, 106; *Queen Mary*, 92, 94; "The Two Voices," 77, 89; "Tithonus," 77

Tennyson, Charles, *Alfred Tennyson*, 157

Tennyson, Hallam, Lord, 155-56; *A Memoir*, 90, 91, 96, 155-56; *The Works of Alfred Lord Tennyson*, 156
Theatre of the Absurd, 159
Theatre of Cruelty, 22, 159
Toynbee, William, *The Diaries of William Charles Macready*, 157
Trelawny, Edward John, *The Recollections of Shelley and Byron*, 152

Viebrock, Helmut, 151
Voltaire (François Marie Arouet), 15

Wagner, Richard, *Ueber die Bestimmung der Oper*, 144
Watson, Ernest B., *Sheridan to Robertson*, 150
"Well-made" play (*pièce bien faite*), 9, 10, 12, 94, 101, 122, 123, 141,

157; and *A Blot in the 'Scutcheon*, 112-21
White, Newman Ivey, *Shelley*, 153
Whitman, Robert F., 153
Wigan, Alfred, 90
Wilkinson, D. C., 158
Wilmot, Mrs. Barbarina, afterwards Baroness Dacre, *Ina*, 43
Wilson, Edmund, *Axel's Castle*, 155
Wilson, Milton Thomas, *Shelley's Later Poetry*, 152
Wolfe, Humbert, *Tennyson*, 156
Wordsworth, William, 91-92; *Borderers, The*, 30; Preface to *Lyrical Ballads*, 144

Yeats, William Butler, 149

Zola, Emil, 77; Preface to *Therésè Raquin*, 144